TALES FROM THE
VICARAGE

TALES FROM THE VICARAGE

A collection of writing inspired
by Watford Football Club

Volume Five
Edited by Lionel Birnie

TALES FROM
www.talesfrom.com

First published in Great Britain in 2016
by Tales From

Printed and bound by SS Media

ISBN 978-0-9932381-4-7

Tales From Ltd
2 Gaddesden Lane, Redbourn, St Albans, AL3 7NP
Registered company number: 9082738

www.talesfrom.com
info@talesfrom.com

TALES FROM THE VICARAGE

CONTENTS

INTRODUCTION

BY THE EDITOR

For the first time in three decades, Watford survived a season among English football's elite, avoiding relegation on their third visit to the Premier League. The Hornets reached the semi-final of the FA Cup for only the sixth time in their history too, making the 2015-16 season one of the most successful campaigns of all time.

This edition of *Tales from the Vicarage* looks back at Quique Sanchez Flores's only season in charge, as well as delving into the past to put Watford's mid-table finish into its proper historical context.

Because, no matter how bright the future appears, football fans can never truly know what is in store. At the moment, we are being encouraged to dream of a sustained spell among the elite, perhaps a shot at winning a trophy or a European tour, but it would be wrong to expect success as some sort of right.

What matters is that the current era is giving us memories to cherish in coming years and, hopefully, *Tales from the Vicarage* is beginning to grow into a series that, when re-read in future, reflects the times we are currently witnessing.

I hope you enjoy this varied collection of stories, written by journalists, broadcasters and former players.

Lionel Birnie

1

Having won promotion, Watford's first move was to replace Slavisa Jokanovic, the man who led them to the Premier League.

Under Quique Sanchez Flores, the Hornets survived in the top flight for the first time in almost 30 years. They also reached an FA Cup semi-final, although before the season was even over, both parties had decided it was time for a change.

Peter Jenson travelled to Barcelona, where Quique took on his next challenge as coach of the city's second club, Espanyol, to find out what the Spaniard made of his time at Vicarage Road.

QUIQUE

BY PETER JENSON
AND LIONEL BIRNIE

The sky in Barcelona on an early autumn day is an uncustomary grey but there's plenty of fire in a full-blooded session at Espanyol's 'Cuitat Esportiva Dani Jarque' training ground.

Quique Sanchez Flores has embraced a new challenge and is back in La Liga after a season in the Premier League, which gave him a taste of English football that he would like to repeat one day.

In summer 2015, and not for the first time, the pundits were scratching their heads at Watford's refusal to comply with the tried and tested way of doing things in English football – and that is sacking coaches only when things have gone wrong.

Few could understand why Slavisa Jokanovic, who had created an exciting, attacking but disciplined side and steered them to promotion was not being given a crack at the top flight.

Less than twelve months on, many were wondering what more Jokanovic's successor could have done, having ensured survival with a greater degree of comfort than many supporters perhaps appreciated. They were used to sitting on the edge of their seats, biting their nails, and were braced for a last-minute brush with relegation, even though mathematics and history urged them to stop fearing the worst. There was an FA Cup run to the semi-finals but that ended with a familiar flat performance against Crystal Palace at Wembley.

But the fact remains that Watford fans had rarely had it so

good. In fact, anyone under the age of 30 had never had it so good, although as the season petered out amid suspicions that Sanchez Flores was too wedded to an inflexible system, too defensive and too reliant on playing people out of position.

Patience is not a virtue in great supply in the Premier League and, like the Roman Emperors of old, the thumb wavered horizontal for a few weeks in the spring before turning down-wards and sealing Quique's fate.

History will perhaps judge his season in charge more kindly and will focus on the thrilling highs, of which there were plenty, rather than the static performances in the final third of the season.

Expectations at the outset were simply to survive. To expect anything more was ridiculous, despite the scale of investment in the team during the summer, which brought in players with Premier League experience. A cautious start brought to the surface fears that this was to be no more than a repeat of the doomed campaigns under Graham Taylor and Aidy Boothroyd. Successive goalless draws against West Brom and Southampton and a display at Manchester City that was devoid of any sign of ambition caused concern. But, as Sanchez Flores explains, there was a reason for those slightly tentative baby steps.

Watford settled and then began to express themselves. After beating Swansea, the pygmies of the Premier League went to Newcastle and slayed the self-styled giants with two goals from Odion Ighalo.

It was the form of Ighalo – who scored more goals in English football than anyone else in 2015 – and Deeney that caught the eye. Ighalo served up his trademark scoops, some-times two at a time. Deeney bullied defenders and showed no deference for the badges on his opponents' chests.

From late October to Christmas, Watford went on a dizzy-ing run of six wins in eight and should have beaten Chelsea at

Stamford Bridge on Boxing Day too. Sanchez Flores was a cool presence on the touchline with a designer wave in his hair, the neat beard with just a hint of grey and a V-neck sweater that suited him far better than it ever suited Vialli. On *Match of the Day,* Ian Wright described him as the 'new sheriff in town', which was a rare comment from a pundit we could all agree with.

The highlights kept coming as the nights drew in. A tense but brilliant away victory at Aston Villa, whose supporters were so sure their struggling season was about to spark into life, was made unnecessarily nerve-wracking when Heurelho Gomes got injured and was replaced by Giedrius Arlauskis, who did his best impression of a circus juggler at times. Norwich were brushed aside, just as West Ham had been. Sunderland were undone by an early Ighalo goal and could not find a way through Watford's resolute defence.

And then came the finest result and performance by Watford in the top flight since the days of Graham Taylor (the first time round, although an honorable mention must also go to the win at Anfield in 1999). Jürgen Klopp's Liverpool were still were still Brendan Rodgers's Liverpool when they visited Vicarage Road a week before Christmas, but don't let that detract from the performance or the result. They came dressed like eleven Santas but they didn't give too many presents. Watford, again inspired by their front two, took them apart and reached Christmas in seventh place.

Who didn't close their eyes, clasp their hands together and wish for a place in the Europa League for 2016 at that stage?

In hindsight, the second half of the season was always going to be more difficult, not necessarily because opponents 'worked them out', (whatever that means) but because Sanchez Flores had relied on such a small group of players and it seemed unlikely they'd be able to keep up the pace. The Premier

League has a habit of handing out the occasional cruel blow. In the first half of the season, there were relatively few bleak moments that left you winded at the injustice of it all. Allan Nyom channelled his inner Marco Cassetti to trip Wilfried Zaha in the penalty area and Deeney bundled the ball into his own net in the last moments against Manchester United having only just scored an equaliser from the spot. Only Arsenal dished out a footballing lesson with a flurry of goals in the second half after the Hornets had played so well for an hour.

Over the Christmas and New Year period, when Watford's compact group of first-teamers were stretched to breaking point, they suffered successive disappointments, against Tottenham and then against Manchester City, where two very late goals overturned a one-nil lead and brought back horrible memories of Premier League seasons past.

After that, they looked tired and uninterested at Southampton, then tired, uninterested and hopeless at Swansea.

By now, though, an FA Cup run was just beginning, with a beautiful victory at the City Ground against Nottingham Forest in round four. This, courtesy of a last gasp goal from substitute Odion Ighalo proved that Watford had arrived in the Premier League as they handed out precisely the kind of undeserved defeat we'd been on the receiving end of many a time. Of course there were rumblings among the faithful that a cup run would lead to a stunning collapse in league form but there's little evidence to suggest that one caused the other.

Having said that, the league form evaporated. As ever, the panacea was sitting on the bench or in the stands, ludicrously overlooked by the head coach, who only has a week's worth of training sessions upon which to judge his players. The yearning for something different was understandable, particularly as the likes of José Manuel Jurado consistently failed to turn his delicate touch and quick feet into something meaningful like, you know, goals and assists.

The grumbling continued as Watford went on a run of six matches without a victory that was every bit as turgid as the opposite streak in the autumn had been exhilarating. And yet had Watford's supporters realised that the point earned in a dreary League One-esque goalless draw against Bournemouth was the one that actually guaranteed safety perhaps the mood would not have been so bleak.

By then it was really all about the FA Cup run. Some assumed that a date at the Emirates Stadium (confirmed very late because of Champions League commitments and other fixture clashes) meant a certain exit. Others still feared that taking the cup seriously would inevitably lead to a slip through the relegation trapdoor, elbowing Norwich, Sunderland, Newcastle and all the other clearly-worse-than-us candidates out of the way. Others still suggested that the FA Cup was so devalued it wasn't worth bothering with. Regarding that one, let's win it and get a replica made for the trophy cabinet before deciding the FA Cup is beneath us, shall we?

Anyway, the victory at Arsenal was glorious. Mike Walters's chapter deals with it in much more detail but even for Watford supporters who lived through the 1980s and all that brought must have felt their hearts bursting out of their chests that afternoon as 9,000 like-minded souls fretted, hid their eyes and then celebrated as if they'd actually won the cup. Okay, so the semi-final was only a marginal improvement on the performance against Palace in the play-off final a few years earlier, but to have the excitement of a cup run to ease the growing frustration of the league campaign was more than merely papering over the cracks.

Even the final weeks, when things began to flat-line, had their moments. A double penalty save by the heroic Gomes at The Hawthorns secured three points that made doubly sure of survival, and seeing Troy Deeney score two very late goals to ram the mocking chants from the Villa fans back down their throats carried a certain satisfaction. After all, we've been in Villa's position before – bound for relegation and all over an opponent who assumed they were safe and had one eye on the beach (or more likely the shopping malls of Dubai these days) only to lose in dramatic circumstances.

Before the season was out, we knew Quique was too. The reception he got on the final day of the season reflected the feelings of the majority of Watford's supporters. He had done something that no manager other than Graham Taylor has ever achieved – he'd survived the top flight. Not only that but he'd done so comfortably.

Some supporters were frustrated by what they perceived as persistence with a favoured system, and particularly with favoured personnel, but the easiest thing in football is to assume that Something Different will be Something Better.

We will never know if perceptions would have been different had the fixtures fallen a different way and the streak of victories had happened in the spring rather than the autumn. Perhaps then, Quique would have been invited to stay for a second year.

But what is clear about the Pozzo model is that a head coach is not necessarily required to become part of the furniture. They do the job they were hired to do and then they move on, and that is what Sanchez Flores has done.

We don't know how the next 12 months will go, let alone the next five years, but if things continue to go well, we'll look back at Quique's season as a first crucial step towards establishing Watford in the Premier League. He steadied the ship, plugged a few leaks and steered it round the icebergs lurking in the Premier League's unfriendly waters and that achievement should not be underestimated or under appreciated.

Yes, there were moments of mind-numbing pragmatism but as newcomers that was exactly what was required at the time. Besides, if the price for hammering Liverpool and beating Arsenal on their own turf, or for arriving at any match, home or away, with a genuine sense that victory could be within our grasp, was to sit through the occasional stinker then it was a price worth paying. After all, who wouldn't have taken 13th place and a cup semi-final had it been on offer in August?

At the end, Watford and Quique went in different directions. The Hornets hope that will lead them to 'the next step'. Quique headed for Espanyol, a club that exists in the rather daunting shadow of city rivals Barcelona.

Tales from the Vicarage had the opportunity to send journalist Peter Jenson to Espanyol's training ground to find out how Sanchez Flores reflected on his time at Watford.

Lionel Birnie

AN INTERVIEW WITH QUIQUE

How did you come to be Watford head coach?

They wanted a meeting with me in Madrid and that took place with [Gino] Pozzo and with agents and with myself and they explained to me what kind of project they wanted. But it wasn't a meeting in an interview sense to see if I was right for the job – it was a meeting to offer me the position.

So somebody had recommended them to you?

I imagine so. There were agents and consultants. And they had the decision pretty much made when we met. The Premier League was a big step for me. It was a dream I'd had for a long time to work in the Premier League so I took the opportunity.

Did they impose an objective for the season and a style of

football that they wanted you to play?
An objective yes, a style of play no. The objective was very clearly marked out – we had to stay up. That was very important for the club. We had to solidify things in that first year and then push on to other challenges that we had met with success at other big clubs such as Atletico Madrid and Valencia.

But there was no desire to play a certain way?
There were questions from the owner about how we wanted to work and what we were going to need to take things forward. We talked about a lot of things so that all our ideas were clear.

Is it fair to say that you would not have known too much about Watford before?
I knew that Elton John had taken over the club in the past and led them up to the top division. I knew they had become a force in the Eighties with players like John Barnes and Luther Blissett. That's an era of football that I love. But it was an interesting project for me. My first job was to find out everything about the club. I went to the training ground and the more I saw the more I realised that Watford was going to be a really interesting challenge for me. It was also something relatively new because it was only the second time in my career I had taken over a team that had just won promotion. I had only done it once before with Getafe 12 years before. I was just 39 years old then and it was the club's first season ever in the top flight. I was more used to taking over teams who were already competing in European competition.

Is it tougher or do you benefit from the positivity around a newly-promoted club?
That's definitely the plus side that everyone is feeling very positive after promotion. You have to take advantage of that feeling

and turn it into something powerful that helps you compete at the higher level.

How did the squad look before the season started?

Before signing the contract we looked out two or three studies of the squad just to know exactly what we were taking over. I looked at five or six games from the previous season, how the team played the previous season and I thought about how we wanted them to play. And on the basis of that we reached an agreement with the owner Gino Pozzo and the two directors of football on what was going to be the foundation for the new season – the players we were going to build the team around, the players who needed to stay at the club and what we needed to bring in.

And you took the decisions over new signings or they were shared?

Always shared, and I mean that in a good way. They asked for my opinion and then four or five options were put before me for each position that we wanted to reinforce and then those names went through a filter. We put the players' names in order of preference and then the club tried to get the first choice and if that was not possible then the second or third and so on. It was impossible to always bring in the first choice, sometimes it was the second or third because the budget had its limits.

Two directors of football must have made things twice as complicated at times?

No because they both went very much in line with the ideas of Gino Pozzo, so it's really Gino Pozzo taking the decisions and he would share with me all the final decisions. It's a very specific model and I was a part in the process. For example, we had to choose between Étienne Capoue and the player who ended up

joining Paris Saint-Germain from Spurs [Benjamin Stambouli].
At one point, we were between this player, Capoue and Valon
Behrami and we had to choose two of the three.

**Off the pitch how was the settling-in process? Where did
you live?**
We lived in Hampstead. It was perfect. It felt like living in a
village surrounded by parkland. We were close to Hampstead
Heath, I was able to go running every day. But I loved the English culture in general. I loved the organisation and the good
manners. And not just in football but also outside of the game
there is a sense that things are well ordered. I valued the experience a lot from that perspective and I valued hugely the way the
fans were towards me. They were always very respectful. That
seemed to be the way it was throughout the country – that is
how they understand football. But at Watford, right from the
first moment, they got behind me and I felt that I had their full
support.

**And that support was there for all to see in the last game
against Sunderland?**
Yes but I felt it all season long. And at the end there was a
feeling that the supporters thought that we should have carried
on; that we deserved to be able to take things on. I value that
hugely.

**And going back to the very first game what are the mem-
ories of Everton?**
We knew it was going to be a difficult start but we had had a
good pre-season, a well-organised pre-season and so we were
ready. And we knew that we were going to be a very well-organised team. And we were closer to winning the game than just
drawing it. We took the lead twice and it was only three or four

minutes from time that they equalised.

And that game was against Roberto Martinez – a friendly enemy on the opening day?

Yes I spoke with him in the traditional post-match meeting between the two coaches. The managers in England nearly always
invite you to have a cup of tea or a glass of wine with them after the game [not something that happens in Spain]. You don't
always have time when the press conferences go on but I met
with quite a few after games. I remember with Slaven Bilic and
Alan Pardew for example. With Eddie Howe also. It happened
a lot of times – with Pochettino and also with Jürgen Klopp.

Klopp had a drink with you even after you beat his Liver-pool team 3-0?

Yes. He was worried that the team didn't really look anything
like the kind of side he wanted. But I told him that he had only
just arrived a couple of weeks before and it was very different
for him. I told him: 'In a couple of months you will have the
players better prepared for what you want from them and you
will have new players that you don't have now.' I told him not
to worry too much.

It's a game that Watford supporters will not forget.

It wasn't just a 3-0 it was a 3-0 that we really deserved. I think
it was the best period of the season. We thought we were capable of anything. And we played a very complete game against
Liverpool. It was perhaps the best performance of the season.

Before that, you'd had to wait a few weeks for the first win, against Swansea...

We could see that win coming. We played Manchester City in
the previous game and we lost 2-0 after two nil-nils [against

West Brom and Southampton]. City came into the game having chalked up big wins in previous games so I put out a side that would not be beaten heavily. We knew it would be very difficult to win the game but we wanted to defend well, to not be too exposed and then having the foundation of a good defensive performance to then go and win our next game against Swansea and that is how it happened. We lost 2-0 to City but they didn't hurt us too much and that really reinforced us and we got the first win in the next game.

And you were the 'new sheriff in town!'
Yes, the new sheriff! People sent me Whatsapp messages at the time along those lines – me as the sheriff. It showed that not just me but also my team was doing a good job. But we know how football is. You have a good moment and you are lined up to be the new Arsenal coach and then you lose the next match and you are lined up for the sack! Hahahah!

When you go to a new country are you very switched on to what kind of impression you are making in the media?
Honestly I can say 'no'. I'm 51 now. When I was a player I always used to read the papers. Then as a coach in the early days I read them but now no, almost never. I love football and I'm interested in what's happening in the world of football but I don't have the time or the necessary dedication to read what is being said about me. I have my family, my children, my life. I like going to the cinema. You have to disconnect.

Were you able to make the most of living in London by going to the cinema, theatre etc?
I would go to the cinema, I would go for walks in London or go to a museum. But above all I would take advantage of the parks just to go for a walk or a run. And there were plenty of

good restaurants too.

So you are not with the players coming to England from abroad who say the food is bad?
No, in London that is not the case. It is a marvellous city. I knew it before as a visitor but to live there was marvellous.

The key to the good start was the partnership between Odion Ighalo and Troy Deeney?
They were both here before we arrived but they had never scored that many goals. We wanted the team to pass the ball a little bit more; we wanted more passes than we had seen in the games in the previous season. But we could not ignore the fact that the team had two strikers who had such a good under-standing. Any direct pass, Deeney could hold it up, and Ighalo would arrive and we could gain 40 metres in just a couple of passes. So we wanted to take advantage of that.

And the team played really well in the first half of the sea-son so that what happened in the second half of the season was that we reached our objectives very quickly. Sincerely I think that we reached the point of safety very soon and we started to think very soon about the chance of doing something big in the FA Cup very early too.

We were in the quarter-finals against Arsenal and I think with that [safety secured before the quarter-final] we allowed ourselves to be distracted. We weren't focusing on things in the same way in the second half of the season as we were in the first half and with that we lost something of the essence of what made us so combative and difficult to play against in the first five months.

So it was difficult to find a new objective when the aim of staying up had been reached?

It's difficult but it shouldn't be like that. You are a professional and you have a good group around you. It should be like that. But it's possible; we are human. And it's also true that it does not help when you have a squad of 22 different nationalities. If you have that and then you get in the situation that we got ourselves into [the season's target met early] finding a challenge that was greater than just survival was difficult.

So the Arsenal game in the FA Cup was the peak of the season?
It was very special. It was an important moment because we had reached Wembley – the chance to play on such a fabulous stage and we were in touching distance of the final. And for Watford to be back at Wembley in the FA Cup final for the first time in so many years would have been marvellous.

We were so close to that and one of the few things that I did not like about my time at Watford was that I did not see any great joy among the directors. I never saw any joy at having reached the semi-final. The fans were happy to be at Wembley, the staff were happy, the players were happy. But among the directors of the club I never saw any desire to live those moments with joy and intensity considering it was something historic. I never saw it. We had secured survival so I never really knew what to read into that. That was a big disappointment for me. That was when my head started to separate from the idea of continuing at Watford – knowing that the club is unable to enjoy historic moments then, as I understand it, what more can you do?

So you had doubts about continuing before they began to have doubts about keeping you?
Yes. I begin to doubt when, three months before the end of the season, something happens that has never happened before.

The owner stops appearing at the club for three months. It was a clear sign to me that this was not the direction I had hoped for. Long before the semi-final, when Watford has done what it needed to do, the directors of the club disappear. They have no presence at the club. From then on the experience starts to disappoint me.

And that affected the atmosphere around the club around the semi-final?
It is bound to. The players know that there is no direction. There is a sense of being abandoned. There are no orders coming down the line. It all depends on what the coach says and there is no support beyond that. We are not all tuned in together anymore.

Do you come to question why they are involved in football if not for these moments?
These are things that I don't understand. I'm in football for the love of it. I'm passionate about the game. I don't know how to work coldly, pessimistically and without enjoying positive achievements. I don't like building things from cold reason alone.

So the feeling around the club is very different to the atmosphere in January?
We brought in Nordin Amrabat, Mario Suarez and Costel Pantilimon and everything was going well. We started off with the objective of playing in a league of four and we had to be top of that league of four [finish 17th]. Every single bookmaker had us as candidates for the drop.

And the other three in that four? Did they go down?
Not exactly because Newcastle went down in the end. The

three teams that came up were the three expected to go down. But what happened is we did not end up in a league of four, we ended up in a league of ten or of 12 and in that league of 12 we finished seventh. I never understood that disconnection. It affected me because the foundation of my work is passion. And I don't understand how others can lose that passion that are working on the same project.

Were there other reasons for the defeat to Crystal Palace in the cup?
We were not at our best on the day. Twenty two different nationalities, and we stopped being a great team and became just a team. Which for me is not enough. Especially when you are a humble side – you need to have a great team mentality.

Was there discord over the system? Did you feel the fans wanted you to verge away from 4-4-2?
I don't think that came from the fans. I think it was more an internal discussion within the club and more to do with the philosophy of the club. They were more accustomed to play with a back three or five, as in the year they went up. But if I'm using 4-4-2 and the results are good why am I going to take a chance? It's also not true that we never varied the formation. We played 4-1-4-1. We played 4-2-3-1 – so there were variations of the principal system. We even played 4-5-1. What we never did was make a big change to a defence of three or to a 4-3-3. But we were flexible.

So the last weeks of the season were difficult because you knew you were going.
There was a deadline to say whether or not we would be staying or not. We had a one year plus one clause in the contract and we had to make that decision on May 21. But, before talking,

we knew there would be no second year. I didn't want to stay somewhere where I understand that things were not going to be done in a way that I liked. So for me the decision was made. And there was a meeting later on when we sat down to talk but clearly my decision had been made before and probably the decision of the club had also already been made. We were agreed on that.

So how did you face the final games?
With the maximum amount of professionalism and trying to pick up the most points possible. And we won games. We beat Aston Villa and we played very well against Liverpool although we lost 2-0. We played well against Manchester United when we lost 1-0 in the 86th minute.

Did the reaction of the fans towards you on the last day surprise you?
Fantastico! But no, it didn't surprise me because it had been that way all year. The support from the fans had been coming from the beginning. They knew I had coached big clubs such as Atletico Madrid, Benfica and Valencia before but they recognised that I was working hard with a lot of humility and a lot of effort.

What is the Quique Sanchez Flores philosophy of football and life?
In football terms I believe in having a method, in organisation and surrounding myself with people who can help me. Sharing the workload in a very ordered way. And to have very committed players who understand the way we want to play. Above all, players who give everything. I can't stand players who don't love their jobs. And in my personal life I like to do a lot of things and to do them wherever I'm living. I love many

different sports, both playing them and watching them. I love cinema, theatre, reading, music, travel. I have a lot of hobbies and I like to keep them up wherever I'm working.

And when you read, you read about football?
No, not necessarily. I read autobiographies. I read books about leadership – *Sacred Hoops* by Phil Jackson [the former Chicago Bulls basketball coach] for example. Biographies of sportsmen or historical figures too. I like reading South American authors such as Mario Benedetti and Gabriel Garcia Marquez. I like to write too. I have written many articles over the years. When I was in that period between being a player and a coach I worked for a lot of newspapers: *Marca*, *AS*, *El Pais*, *El Mundo*. I was lucky enough for them to allow me write about what interested me. I think I wrote over a thousand articles in that time and they are filed somewhere.

Do you have things at home to remind you of Watford?
I have very few things from my entire career. The few things I have are looked after by my loved ones. But I'm not a great collector.

You have the memories...
I have the memories, correct.

How was that phone call with Elton John?
The famous phone call! He called me while I was in central London in a hairdressers with my four children. It was funny. The club told me he was going to call. But I didn't have his number so 'Elton' didn't come up on the phone when he called. It was my turn in the chair and I gave my daughter the phone and she passed it to me saying there was a call from an 'unknown number' and it was Elton John. I exchanged a few

words with him but the hairdresser who was cutting my hair must have thought I was someone important because I was saying: 'yes, Sir Elton; no, Sir Elton' And he soon realised that I was related to the world of football because of the nature of the conversation. Not to be outdone when he'd finished cutting my hair he told me he had recently cut Placido Domingo's hair.

Would you go back to the Premier League?
I would love to. There is so much that I like about it. And I think for the type of coach I am, I'm closer to the Premier League than any other league.

Peter Jenson writes about Spanish football for the *Daily Mail*. He also contributes to *The Independent*, BBC Radio 5 Live and Eurosport.

2

Stuart Hutchison led out the Hornets before a victory over Notts County in December 1979.

He wasn't the captain, of course, but a seven-year-old mascot.

Thirty-six years later, his eldest son was selected for the same honour before the match against Liverpool.

And while young Alex took the occasion in his stride, dad Stuart was nervous – and it wasn't just fretting about keeping up the family's 100 per cent record that was on his mind…

LEADERS OF MEN

BY STUART HUTCHISON

'Hang on! You were, what, SEVEN years old? And they printed your FULL address and house number?'

My friend Kelly from the BBC – displaying a concern for child welfare perhaps not universally shared by all her predecessors at the Corporation – had seen my Facebook post, and raised a valid point.

My eldest son, Alex, had just been a matchday mascot, for the Watford v Liverpool game in December, 2015. The occasion had gone rather well and, in the febrile excitement of the following days, I retrieved the matchday programme from the day when I too, led out the Golden Boys – a slightly less emphatic 2-1 (Blissett, Bolton) slaying of Notts County in the run-up to Christmas, 1979.

I put the photos of us leading the teams out, 36 years apart, and screenshots of our respective mentions in the programmes, on Facebook.

'This is brilliant. What a thing for a father & son to have done.'
'I love this!'
'This is great! Why did you keep it such a secret!'
'Hang on! You were, what, SEVEN years old? And they printed your FULL address and house number?'

Abject failure on the pitch sends supporters scurrying into a warren of warm, comforting nostalgia for better times, so over the years the visits to my mum's loft have been many and frequent. And while there I always seek out my name printed in the programme from that otherwise quite unremarkable Football League Division Two encounter, but this was the first time I'd done so in the current climate – and by 'climate', I mean the unending hurricane of celebrity scandals that had drastically reduced the public's appetite for a return of *Summertime Special.*

And there it was, inside the back cover, sandwiched between details of the referee – 'a married man, with two sons' – and notification of the next home fixture at Vicarage Road against Sunderland.

Stuart Hutchison (7),
house number, road name, Garston, Herts.

As I'm sure you'll agree, a somewhat unnecessary level of detail. They might as well have added: 'is largely left unattended on Tuesdays between four and five-fifteen'.

Those were, of course, more innocent times. Or perhaps less innocent. In any case, football clubs now stick to the solid 'Hobbies, Favourite Player, Score Prediction' format. And this isn't the only way the Watford mascot experience has changed over the past 30-odd years.

It started with a letter, back then. I found it while I was looking for the programme.

> *Dear Stuart,*
> *Thank you very much indeed for applying for the position of Mascot to the Watford Team for season 1979-80.*
> *As you will have seen in the Press Release, we intend to have two mascots for each home match, and I am delighted to say that you have been allocated to the match versus Notts County on 1/12/79.*
> *We are all looking forward to making your acquaintance at*

*this particular time, and would ask you to bring with you this letter
to the Home Team dressing room where I look forward to meeting
you. Please bring with you your football boots and plenty of good
luck!*

Best wishes,
Graham Taylor

Typical of the man – though I accept the probability that
his secretary may have had a hand in it; Graham was busy
writing The Greatest Story Ever Told at the time – and typical
of the club in the late 1970s and early 1980s as well.

This time, we got an e-mail from the club and, although less
personal, I'm happy and proud to report that at no point during
Alex's big day was the personal touch missing.

The first person we met – or rather, 'engulfed' – was Luther
Blissett, taking in the low winter lunchtime sun as he strolled
the perimeter of his former domain. As we hurried behind to
catch him up, I fished around in Alex's goody bag for a little
book and pen.

Autograph hunting. Now here's the thing. Boil it down to
the absolute fundamentals – so all the peripheral elements of
it evaporate away – and what you've got left is the very essence
of it. And what that essence is, is this:

I want you to write down your name for me.

It is just that. It's like triple-jumping. Strip away the records,
the competition, the sponsorship money, and the nuts and bolts
of this silly business is a person who, when asked what he/she
does for a living, would, if they were being true to themselves,
have to simply reply: 'I run, then I hop onto this foot, then I do
a jump onto the other foot, then I land in some sand.' Imagine
explaining that.

So I've always struggled to see the point of autograph hunting. And anecdotal evidence suggests I'm not alone. A friend

and colleague has been in the privileged position to potentially see all manner of famous people write down their names for him, but has always said no. Except once. A few years back he found himself at a press junket fronted by Pele. Each journalist was given a New York Cosmos football shirt and a beautiful, leather retro New York Cosmos holdall in their famous olive green colours.

My colleague thought, well, the bag will be great for the gym but the shirt... and after all it IS Pele...

So he asked The Great Man to sign the shirt for him, thinking that it would look nice framed on the study wall. He turned away, and looked back to see the old fella zoning in on the holdall with marker pen in hand.

NOT THE BAG, PELE!!!

The whole room stopped and stared, as a very sheepish, gentle old Greatest Footballer Who Ever Lived, looked at his feet and said: "You're the first person to ever ask me NOT to sign something."

My friend's reasoning, of course, was that a New York Cosmos holdall autographed by Pele wouldn't last ten seconds in the light-fingered locker rooms of Sheffield. He tells me happily, however, that a New York Cosmos holdall with a big black letter P scrawled on it, is less of a target for thieves.

Anyway, within seconds, Luther was cornered. Backed into the Elton John seats by a slavering pack of dads brandishing autograph books and yellow club biros, while their children stood back, clutching what remained of their mascot gift bags.

Eventually, we let them meet him too.

For the parents, the day had almost peaked already. For the mascots, it got significantly more exciting as Rene Gilmartin and Tommy Hoban kicked off a rolling cast of meeters-and-greeters in front of the tunnel.

No seat on the bench remained unoccupied, no inch of

tunnel wall unphotographed.

'Alex, would you like your photo taken with some of the Liverpool players? Some of them play for ENGLAND!!'

'No. Just Watford players.'

This delighted me for two reasons. One, I've never really GOT patriotism. So you happened to be born in the same country as me, did you? And this means I am somehow obliged to support you in all your endeavours, does it? Hmmm. Sounds flimsy to me. And, frankly, if you'd watched the movie *Independence Day* in a cinema in America and found your head engulfed by billowy pillows of tummy as the men either side of you high-tenned each other to celebrate Will Smith flying his thing into the galactic wotsit, you'd hate irrational country-love as well.

And secondly, my children, as is the custom in Bushey, are brought up in strict accordance with Marxist doctrine. Alex knows that the natural division of mankind is not nationality, but class. The struggle of which is the true motor of history.

And he also knows that Jordan Henderson is a bit shit.

Another great German who could teach mankind a thing or two about how to treat one other, strolled past.

'Excuse me. No, sorry, not you. Herr Klopp… would you mind stopping for a photo with my son please?'

As befitting a man who had just set foot inside the Premier League bubble and had yet to learn the code of conduct, Jürgen Klopp could not have been more polite and smiley.

While Alex did shuttle runs of the technical area in preparation for his kickabout on the pitch with the other mascots, I reviewed the photos and noticed my son was, ahem, 'holding himself' in every picture. An unsuccessful visit to the toilet suggested the lad was suffering from big-match nerves. And who, frankly, could blame him? I couldn't. On my 'big' day, a small crowd of single-figure thousands watched me lead out

The Hornets. The media coverage consisted of Oliver Phillips of the *Watford Observer*, and perhaps a stringer from the *Sunday People*. This contrast dawned on me as the Sky TV Steadicam operator rehearsed one of his 'teams out' moves by slaloming backwards around Alex, while a decent veterans XI of famous old faces stood by in expensive shoes waiting to discharge their various global media duties, and the first of the 20,000 fans began to filter in, to find giant banners prepared in three of the stands.

I remember Dennis Booth's arse and I remember Luther cannoning a ball off the white breeze block wall in the long treatment area that adjoined the dressing room. By anyone's standards, this is a disappointing harvest of recollections. There is a good reason for this.

I have a photograph, taken by the *Watford Observer* photographer on duty that day in 1979, and it was taken as the teams emerged from the tunnel. Booth, now clothed, is in the middle of the shot, with Keith Mercer, Eric Steele and Luther behind him. My dad is to the right of the tunnel, smoking a cigar (don't get many of those at football these days), and on the other side is a policeman (nor them). In front of the Watford skipper are me and my fellow mascot, Jason Rose (7), house number, road name, Watford, Herts.

Jason is looking at me excitedly, and gives the impression that he's taking it all in. I'm looking down at the floor. And guess what I can remember of leading out my heroes.

I remember the gravel. I remember the gravel and the cinder-coloured stones that used to ring the pitch. I remember walking across it, and as soon as brown gives way to green in my mind's eye, that's where the video ends. I remember nothing else about the day, even though the matchday programme informs me – and my mum confirms this as an eye-witness – I warmed-up pre-kick-off with substitute John Ward (in those days the final minutes before 3pm weren't cluttered with empty gestures of fair play conducted in front of a flimsy arch upon which words conjured by the marketing department of a face-less multinational corporation lecture the crowd on the spirit of the game), and the match itself was notable for one of the Notts County players getting sent-off AT HALF TIME for complaining too much to the referee about a penalty decision.

So I told Alex to savour it, remember every moment. And to stop holding himself.

I later realised how nerveless he had been. Not only not holding himself but... he had told Troy Deeney where to stand.

For the entrance of the teams, the parents are taken over to the hospital-side touchline, in order to get a good look at the mascots and to collect them when they run off before kick-off. As I explained before, my mind's 'video' of my big day pretty much ended as soon as I stepped out of tunnel. For that reason, plus the expectation that my own iPhone camerawork would be poor AND that there would be insufficient Alex in the SKY TV coverage obsessed with 'the players' and 'the football', I'd decided that afterwards, I would make a lasting reminder of the occasion. I would nip into my former place of work, the BBC, and collect all the angles of Alex from all the Sky cameras, and make my own 'Director's Cut' of Watford v Liverpool. And when I found the footage from the tunnel camera, which started filming ten minutes before kick off, this is what I saw.

The mascots have left the dressing room and are waiting in a line in the tunnel. Alex was due to walk out with his favourite, Heurelho Gomes. The dressing room door swings open and Troy Deeney emerges to shake hands with referee Mark Clattenburg, before saying hello to each child.

'Hello young man.'

'You're not with me you're with him.' Alex pointed to the boy in front of him.

'Oh, okay. Er, thanks.'

And in perhaps his only sheepish act of an otherwise swash-buckling, torso-ripping, body-art-exposing season, Troy Deeney filed silently and obediently to the front of the line.

Know your place, Deeney.

Once my son was content that everyone was standing in the right place, formalities could commence.

Alex doesn't like loud noise. To be frank, you'd have to go back to the Catholic underworld of the early 17th Century to find someone less keen on the concept of bonfire night than my eldest son. I was apprehensive about the emergence of the teams, and how he would cope with the wave of sound. The previous 20 years may have been a better time for him to be a Watford supporter. I needn't have worried. From the opening drum flourish of Z-Cars, he coped beautifully. His privates remained untroubled, no Liverpool hand remained unshaken, and he posed for his photo in the centre circle like a professional.

I was also concerned that we wouldn't be able to get him off the pitch. I feared he might go off to take the acclaim of the crowd for successfully not holding his willy for five minutes, thereby delaying the kick-off. But no, he sprinted off into my arms, then as we walked around the pitch, Alex applauding the Rookery in the Paul Robinson-style, we took our usual seats in the Elton John Stand with a couple of minutes of the match played. It was a cold day. The middle of December. I said: 'Alex, we'll get your tracksuit out of the bag in a minute. But just wait a second, we've got a corner…'

The Greatest Day of His Life was only just beginning.

Stuart Hutchison watches Watford FC when working in television doesn't get in the way. He longs for the day The Internet kills the latter, allowing him to devote all his energies to the former.

3

Beppe Sannino arrived when the Zolacoaster had run off the rails. A disciplinarian with an occasional wild flash in his eyes, he was just the man to put the wagon back on track.

Attracted by the passion of English football, Sannino fell in love not just with the game, but with Watford.

But it was to be a brief affair and one that ended just when things appeared to be going perfectly.

Sannino tells **Paolo Tomaselli** what happened and why a little piece of his heart remains in Hertfordshire.

BEPPE

BY PAOLO TOMASELLI

'I had my head down and was saying "sorry, sorry", because we had just lost 4-1 and I was ashamed of the result. They were singing songs with my name, like *Beatles* songs. And they were signalling to me to hold my head up. For me it was an honour, even if I didn't fully understand it, but I applauded and did a lap of the pitch with the players with their children on their shoulders. It was the final match of the season, we had lost against Huddersfield, and I was thinking: but how can we go out on to the pitch and face our fans? But they were there, in the stands, along with the opposing fans. This is my favourite among many memories of my experience at Watford. Because it shows the difference between the football I was used to in Italy, and the football I found in England.'

Beppe Sannino's life in Watford was like landing from another planet, or something similar. But above all it was a love story: not long, but intense and passionate, and capable of leaving a fond memory. Both for him – a manager whose career in Italy had been unconventional, and for the people of Watford: 'They fell in love with this wild madman on the bench,' smiles Beppe, 'who tried to drop himself into a completely new reality, without pretending to be different. They made me feel important in a land that wasn't my own.

'And I hope I will be able to experience a match in an English stadium again, even though I've left Watford. Perhaps people don't understand why I left, and now I'm ready to explain. But first I would like to describe one or two things that I saw.'

Indeed this observational capacity has been fundamental for Sannino, who at 57 suddenly found himself in an unknown world, without a command of the language. 'I challenge anyone to try it. I tried to throw myself into it, mistakes and all. But I did it because of the passion I have for my profession. Perhaps that was a little naïve, and maybe I was taken for a ride because I wasn't able to speak [the language]. But I think my stubbornness in wanting to make myself understood might even have made them like me. I could have said I'm only speaking Italian and trusted myself to the translator. But I wanted to touch the players' hearts – to use my tone of voice to make them understand what I wanted them to do. I didn't always succeed, particularly on the psychological level, precisely because of language problems. That's a regret, because a team has the character of its manager. But I had the strength to try it. And also to learn so much, including about personal relationships.'

Before his first match, at Ipswich Town four days before Christmas 2013, he needed to talk to the players straight away in the dressing room. Sannino had brought Marco Cesarini with him, whose job it was to translate the manager's thinking, at least at the start. So he started the pre-match talk in Italian, but used a difficult-to-translate expression which would sound a bit complicated even in a Serie A dressing room: '*ci accingiamo*' ['we are on the point of…']. And his translator found himself in difficulty, because he couldn't find the exact words in English. It all ended in laughter. Thanks also to the dressing room tendency to play things down: 'In Italy there is a lot more pre-match tension. They listen to music [in England], whatever they want, really loud. Not like in Italy where there's a religious silence and everyone has their headphones on. Post-match is also much more calm in England. For me, losing is physically painful; while there, they taught me to digest the defeat straight away: in the first match of the second year we lost 3-0 to Norwich and I was really pissed off. "Why are you sad?" they said. "Let's concentrate on the next match." That would be inconceivable in Italy.'

So how did Beppe Sannino come to be at Watford? It so happened that Zola was having problems, and the Pozzos' trusted lawyer Vagheggi contacted the manager, who had a few days earlier been released from Serie A's Chievo Verona (after a 0-0 draw against Milan). The meeting with Gino Pozzo took place in Mestre, close to Venice, and ended well: 'When I arrived in Watford, nobody knew me,' says Beppe. 'But they found themselves a person who knew how to be in the world: the only thing they knew about me, as an Italian, was that I had been chosen by the owner and that I was linked to them. Maybe because of that they thought I might be malleable. On YouTube you can see an interview where at one point the journalist uses the term "yes man". That really pissed me off: because you can say anything about my career, but not that anyone has ever walked over me. I have also paid a personal price for this part of my character, and my somewhat unusual journey is there to prove it.'

When Beppe Sannino talks about the training ground and in particular about the stadiums he visited with Watford, you really understand how his passion for football has changed. And that it has become 'a passion for English football'. It's something that is tricky to explain to someone who has not visited Italian football grounds, be that in the lower leagues or in Serie A: remember the tears of Claudio Ranieri, emotional seeing his family in the stands to celebrate his triumphs at Leicester? It is those same emotions that Sannino often felt. But talking about it gives him goose pimples: 'Because we never travelled with a police escort. Because when we got out of the coach, people greeted us, including our opponents. And they asked us for photos and autographs. Because the stands are always full and cheery. Because on the pitch, it's football for men. Because at an event that you had to attend, if there was a long queue of people in the cold and rain, everyone respected that. On the pitch and off it I saw *La Grande Bellezza*.'[1]

Even if all the scenes of the English film are not Oscar-worthy, we would miss him. Because on the road of a foreign manager, one who was not famous, and with demonstrable problems with the language, it's easy to leave the odd trap lying around: 'I remember Redknapp,' Sannino recalls with an amused tone, 'who, before the match against QPR, knowing that I was bald but not knowing me personally, went to shake the hand of De Toffol, the goalkeeping coach. I was to one side, talking to someone, but he pretended not to see me.'

'Respect', together with 'pride', is a key word for the Italian technician. Here, we enter another field: that of the relationship with players in a football that is profoundly different to the Italian game, including in the dressing room. Watford, particularly at that time, however, had a Tricolore soul – Cassetti, Faraoni, Fabbrini, Angella, Forestieri, Battocchio, Pudil and Abdi knew Sannino and helped him.

Marco Cassetti in particular, for his age and experience, was an essential reference point: 'An incredible guy,' Sannino relates. 'He told me straightaway that things on the pitch were tough, particularly in terms of tactics, which is perhaps the aspect of football where we Italians are second to none. I was asked to work in the Italian way and at first I did 4-4-2, then also 5-3-2, even though I'm convinced that defence is best with four. We are very fussy on certain things and we don't put up with poor tactical concentration, which in fact had let us give away a few too many goals in the last few minutes of matches. But English players – if you try to explain too many things to

---

[1] *La Grande Bellezza*, or The Great Beauty is a 2013 Italian film

them, they tell you it's boring. At the end of the day, I tried to
bring a certain tactical discipline but it was exhausting because
the guys want to have fun – for them it's all a game, even when
they lose. On the other hand they are polite, they don't like a
manager who shouts, and they give their heart and soul on the
pitch, pulling out 120 per cent of what they've got. If you ask
them to climb a mountain, they will.'

Other than Cassetti ('who suffered when he left England'),
Almen Abdi and Heurelho Gomes were also leaders in the
dressing room and helped Sannino, explaining things to him
frankly, for example the team's preferred training style: 'short
but very intense'. Other players were important, like Angella
('of English temperament'), Ekstrand ('almost a younger
brother to me'), Fabbrini ('a lover of dribbling, who would
sometimes fall and people would think it was on purpose, but
it wasn't').

Sannino arrived to steady a rocking ship and he certainly
prevented it from capsizing but the season ended with four defeats, culminating with that 4-1 humbling by Huddersfield. The
team finished 13th in the table and Sannino hoped that having
a summer to work with the players might give him the platform
to build a promotion-winning campaign.

On the pitch, the signs were very encouraging. Watford lost
the second game 3-0 at Norwich but the other league games all
ended in victory – 3-0 against Bolton, 2-0 at Rotherham and
4-1 and 4-2 against Leeds and Huddersfield. But not all the
signals were positive and, for a passionate man like Beppe, little
able to mediate, certain situations weighed heavily.

'At Rotherham, we won 2-0. One player made a scene
because he felt too important,' he says, referring to Lloyd Dyer's celebration after scoring, when he ran in front of the bench
and gestured to Sannino at his frustration of not being handed
a starting place following his transfer from Leicester. At the

time, Sannino claimed not to have seen Dyer's emotional outburst but it clearly registered. 'From there, I saw there could be problems,' he says.

There was something quite appropriate about the fact that Sannino's final game came against Huddersfield at Vicarage Road and it atoned for the 4-1 defeat on the last day of the previous season, when Beppe struggled to look the fans in the eye but experienced their support nonetheless. Huddersfield were beaten 4-2, and Sannino's team appeared to be slotting into gear ready for the anticipated promotion push.

But all was not as it seemed. Sannino was honest enough to know he could not go any further on the journey.

'I thought about what the Pozzos had invested in this project. We were second [in the table], one point behind Nottingham Forest, but I couldn't see the necessary composure around me: players arrived who believed they should always be picked for the first team. And there were other controversial gestures, other minor misunderstandings. People didn't understand my choice. But I had to just think of the good of the team. I spoke to Gino Pozzo about it, and he didn't want me to go. By now, however, I'd made my choice, and I resigned. I asked only that things would be settled with my colleagues. I knew that a new face on the bench would be good for Watford, who in fact went on to win promotion. It was right for my work to finish at that point, out of respect for the club, the team and the fans. Is it also down to me what happened afterwards? That's not for me to say. I know that I gave a lot, and got back even more from so many people, which I will always carry in my heart. If I had a second life, I would like to go back, with more experience and greater awareness. To relive particular emotions.'

Paolo Tomaselli is an Italian sports journalist and football writer based in Milan who covers Serie A for the respected daily newspaper *Corriere della Sera*.

4

Simon Burnton looks at how quickly expectations rose following promotion to the Premier League.

The rest of the football world could not understand why Watford released the head coach after he steered the team to a comfortable mid-table finish.

Quique Sanchez Flores oversaw a run to the FA Cup semi-final too, so had the Hornets faithful suddenly got too big for their boots?

Or is it simply a case that the owners' refusal to stand still or settle for stability has transmitted itself to the supporters, who now expect to keep climbing upwards?

A SENSE OF PERSPECTIVE

BY SIMON BURNTON

Home fans headed to Vicarage Road with an air of absolutely logic-free optimism, even though the opponents Leicester were engaged in an ultimately glorious battle at the top of the table and Watford never seemed likely to match them. Anticipation built like sandcastles in Skegness in summertime, and then, as kick-off arrived like a crashing wave, it dissolved.

It hadn't exactly been a season of unfettered glory, though there had been some bright performances, a few thrilling afternoons of stupefyingly carefree attacking, but on this day all that was a ghost, a memory. The defence was largely sturdy, keeping the visitors' lightning-fast English striker under control, but the attack was listless. The performance was leaden, chances few, and when the Foxes' right winger finally scored the only goal of the game, with just under an hour played, reality struck. Defeat was suddenly, undeniably, unavoidable. The remainder of the game was played out with a surprising absence of spirit, and the scoreline remained unchanged, and not seriously threatened, until the final whistle blew.

At which point, the home fans stood as one. And they applauded. 'At the whistle Watford fans rose to Graham Taylor,' wrote John Perlman in the *Independent*. 'Amid the disappointment Vicarage Road acknowledged there was no more he could have done.'

The defeat, in 1996, was the result that sealed Watford's

relegation from what is currently the Championship. Precisely two months short of 20 years later the same clubs played a very similar game at the same venue. Instead of Emile Heskey, Jamie Vardy provided Leicester's pace. Instead of Muzzy Izzet in the 59th minute, Riyad Mahrez was the goalscorer in the 56th. Instead of promotion through the play-offs, the Foxes were on their way to winning the actual, proper league title. Instead of condemning them to relegation to the third tier, the result left Watford 13th in the top flight. And instead of applauding, most of the home fans slipped silently from the stadium, and from the remainder there was as much grumbling as applauding, sometimes both combined.

'The standing ovation at the end,' Andrew Longmore had written in *The Times* in 1996, 'suggested Watford's sense of perspective had not deserted them during a traumatic season.' Where, now, was that sense of perspective?

* * *

It is true that, if you're trying to coax a standing ovation out of a Watford crowd, it very much helps if you're Graham Taylor. He would go on to lead the team to two promotions in the next three seasons, but these were just bonus achievements, successes which poured more goodwill into a cup that was already overflowing. As he strode into the centre circle to acknowledge the fans' support that May afternoon, he could have farted loudly, stolen an infant's teddy and drop-kicked a puppy onto a barbecue and few would have stopped clapping.

It was also true that he could hardly be blamed for Watford's failure that season, having taken over an imploding team from Glenn Roeder in February and having managed to coax an improvement which saw his side win successive home games in April by scores of 5-2, 4-2 and 6-3, all despite having an attack led by Devon White, a man whose footballing reputation stood in inverse proportion to his own giant frame and whose lumbering presence made Craig Ramage, top scorer that season, look like a latter-day Zico. And, as it turned out, even victory on that final day would not have been enough to save the side from relegation. The only thing anyone seemed to have to be cheerful about that day was that, even if Watford only finished above one team that season, at least it was Luton Town. Yet, still, they cheered.

When a group of supporters can take relegation to the third tier, with all the uncertainty it entails, with greater equanimity than they would one day accept a narrow defeat to the best team in the country during a first season back in the top flight, it does prompt a few questions about perspective.

The Premier League game against Leicester came towards the start of a trying run that concluded the 2015-16 season. Watford's last half-dozen home games brought three draws – a 0-0 against Bournemouth in which Heurelho Gomes was the man of the match, a 1-1 against a feeble Everton in which both goals came in 30 seconds at the end of the first half, and a 2-2, having twice fallen behind, against what was more or less the reserve team of nearly-relegated Sunderland on the final day – plus defeats to Leicester and Stoke and a solitary victory, stolen from the jaws of defeat with two goals in the last three minutes, against the ten-man, rock-bottom, morale vacuum that was Aston Villa.

Five of the last six away games were lost, the only exception being the 1-0 victory at West Brom in which Saido Berahino failed to convert either of two penalties and Gomes was man of the match once again.

This was a little uncanny, as the last time Watford were in the top flight, in 2006-07, their last six home games had brought three draws, two defeats and a single win, while away

from home they had lost five of their last six and won the other
(a 2-0 victory at Reading notable mainly for being the first
and final league appearance of Cedric Avinel, who started at
centre-back and was replaced at half-time). On the previous
visit to the top flight, in 1999-2000, their final dozen fixtures
once again featured three draws, two wins and seven defeats,
even if the distribution of the results – both wins were earned
at home, and one draw away – was not quite identical. The difference between those seasons and this was that, with 12 games
remaining, in 2007 Watford were bottom of the table with 18
points, in 2000 they were bottom of the table with 15 points,
and in 2016 they were 14th with 28 points.

This comparison demonstrates two things: firstly, what
Watford witnessed towards the end of the 2015-16 season was
of a standard that, if sustained for much longer than three
months, would almost certainly lead to relegation, and that had
in fact led to relegation twice in the club's recent history. But
also it is not a run of results so poor that should normally
provoke panic in the boardroom.

Following the conclusion of the 1999-2000 campaign
Taylor remained at Vicarage Road, but though the next season
started promisingly – Watford were top with 35 points after 13
games – it tailed off in dismal style and he departed at its end.
Aidy Boothroyd, who led the team through the 2006-07 campaign, also stayed at the club, but though the following season
started promisingly – Watford were top with 32 points after 13
games – it tailed off in similarly dismal style and he departed
another six months later.

Quique Sanchez Flores received no second chances,
despite steering Watford to safety. His imminent departure was
announced with one game still to play, a move that seemed to
prompt less grumbling from Watford supporters than did that
performance against Leicester.

Before what turned out to be Sanchez Flores's final game at the club Watford fans unfurled three giant banners. One, bearing the Spaniard's own face, was lifted in the Family Stand. Another, of Troy Deeney, was passed along the lower tier of the stand now named after Taylor. The third, bigger than both of those put together and then some and raised in the middle of the Rookery End, where the most vocal of the home fans congregate, carried the face, and name, of the club's owner, Gino Pozzo.

Perhaps the lack of uproar caused by Sanchez Flores's uprooting demonstrated not that Watford's supporters were ungrateful, but that they were grateful to someone else. Their support had not disappeared, but been redistributed. Football fans are by their nature loyal types, ready to pledge their troths to anyone who demonstrates any kind of reciprocal loyalty and commitment should they be at all and in any way good. Traditionally they have focused on players and on managers, but by turning the dugout into a spinning carousel of utter unreliability and spending every transfer window ushering players into the club and then out again as if they were lactating cattle at a milking parlour, Pozzo – intentionally or otherwise – created an environment in which the fans were, out of utter necessity, sooner or later going to raise a banner with his face on it and start singing his name.

The Taylor and Boothroyd top-flight seasons proved that by achieving success a manager can win sufficient trust for them to survive a subsequent dip. Slavisa Jokanovic had credit in the goodwill bank after leading the team to promotion in 2015 but a contractual squabble forced him out before he had time to use it, and Sanchez Flores's stay was so brief that, to continue the banking analogy, he had his marching orders before he'd set up his standing orders.

Pozzo, of course, had no need to rig the club's player and

management recruitment policy to ensure the focus fell eventually upon himself. All he had to do in order to be acclaimed was be less abysmal than his immediate predecessor, Laurence Bassini, a target which he has exceeded more emphatically than anyone since Isaac Newton set out to have a nice sit down in an orchard and came home having accidentally discovered gravity. But it is also true that the majority of those in the press box for the match against Sunderland were utterly befuddled by the Pozzo banner.

Of course, there were plenty of reasons other than an owner's ego for ushering Sanchez Flores to the exit. There were the performances, of course, which from January onwards inspired little more than frustration. And there were also issues with man-management. Casey Stengel, the great baseball player and coach who spent the entire 1950s in charge of the New York Yankees, where he won five consecutive World Series titles and seven in all, once said that 'management is a cinch – all you have to do is keep the five guys who hate your guts away from the four guys who haven't made up their minds', and it is a trick that the Spaniard never quite managed.

Most players – there have been a couple of inglorious exceptions – don't much like not playing. If you have only perhaps a dozen years in which to make your mark on the world and somebody denies you one of them for reasons beyond your understanding, there is bound to be a little bitterness. A manager must be above that kind of sentimentality, of course, but he must also be conscious of the implications of his decisions. Sanchez Flores came across as perhaps the most humble and human of recent Watford managers, but seemed simultaneously to be entirely ignorant of these most human of concerns.

When, for example, Steven Berghuis joined the club in August 2015 the player accepted it was 'going to be hard' to keep a place in the first team, but that 'if I show that I am scoring goals… creating chances and giving assists, I think he won't take me out'. It seemed a logical and sensible ambition but the Dutchman never had a first-team place to keep, making just five league appearances, varying in length from six minutes to 26, before April. Adlène Guedioura only once spent more than ten minutes on the pitch in a league game before mid-March (and that runout only lasted 21 minutes).

Victor Ibarbo was trying to rebuild his career after an injury-plagued spell at Roma and would surely never have joined Watford on deadline day in August 2015 had he any inkling that he would see only 64 minutes of first-team football over the next five months, whereupon he was allowed to flee back to his native Colombia. Alessandro Diamanti, a 32-year-old with 17 international caps for Italy, played precisely one more minute before, like Ibarbo, leaving again in January and declaring the experience 'a nightmare'. 'I trained well but never had the chance to show what I can do on the pitch,' he sniffed after joining Atalanta. 'I don't know why I didn't play. I didn't even have a chance, which I would have deserved. It was humiliating and disrespectful towards me.' One imagines those sentiments were fairly widely shared among the non-playing members of Watford's playing squad.

But even so. Even so. More than anything the impression made by Sanchez Flores's departure, and the grumbling on the terraces that preceded it, was that suddenly 13th place in the Premier League, however it happened to be achieved, was not considered good enough.

Yet in the wider football world the reaction to his leaving, which tended to vacillate between bemusement, anger and pity, betrayed the impression that 13th place, however it happened to be achieved, should be enough to have the denizens of WD18 enthusiastically embracing strangers in the street before naming any resulting offspring after their bestubbled Iberian hero.

'It's crazy,' said West Ham's Slaven Bilic. 'I'm sorry for
Quique. It's completely wrong, they've had a fantastic season.
As far as I know if someone had offered Watford that ...
before the season everyone predicted they were likely candidates to go down. Yet they were never in danger and until
January or February they were in the top eight, or top ten. Add
to that they play good football, and add to that they were in the
semi-final of the FA Cup. They had a great season, the place
was buzzing, it was a season to be proud of. It's completely
wrong, it's sick.'

How, though, to explain this divergence of opinion
regarding Sanchez Flores's exit? Outside Watford, everyone
was incredulous; inside, everyone was indifferent. Why? And
what did it all mean?

Perhaps Leicester were to blame. By running away with the
league title they removed from the Premier League its comfort
blanket of predictability. Over a period of years the league had
split into one largely settled group of perhaps six clubs who
might compete for a place in the top four, a further six who
would battle for the four remaining positions in the top half,
and a remaining eight who would be desperately trying not to
get relegated.

It remained possible to switch from one mini-
division to another, but to do so took time, luck and quite
possibly the arrival of a spendthrift oil squillionaire. Under this
system a newly-promoted side who managed to finish 13th
would have effectively won its league, and could stroll off into
the summer sunset wearing a smile of hazy satisfaction.

Suddenly, though, nobody needs to settle. Last season's
last-minute relegation-dodgers can be next season's champions,
all it takes (major simplification alert) is a bit of imagination.
Tottenham's frustration at falling short of winning the league
title in their finest season for generations must have come at

least in part from the fact that, having worn the motto on their shirts for years, when it suddenly turned out that to dare was to do after all, it wasn't them doing the daring or the doing.

So, Watford finished 13th. There are two ways of looking at this situation. One is to be extremely grateful: Luton, chosen not because of their historical rivalry with Watford but because they were until not long ago a vaguely similarly-sized club from a vaguely similarly-sized place in a vaguely similar location who tended to do vaguely similarly, came 11th in League Two, and that was one of their best seasons for some time. There but for the grace of God, and all that. Besides, in an only slightly alternate reality Bassini remains the club chairman and what Watford's current position would be then is a matter for wild and deeply unpleasant conjecture. Watford finished 13th. Be thankful. Regroup. Do it again.

'You don't push on after one season,' said John Barnes after Sanchez Flores was pushed out the *puerta*, quite nicely summing up this point of view. 'A club like Swansea, who've been in the Premier League for maybe four or five years, or Stoke, then you can say, "Now that we've cemented our position in the Premier League, we can now look to be more ambitious." You can't come up, be relegation favourites and because you stayed up, then say, "Let's look to push on." You have to consolidate, regularly finishing in the next four or five years in mid-table – then you can look to push on.'

The other reaction to a 13th-place finish is to replace gratitude with frustration, to aim for more, to dare. For if Leicester proved in 2015-16 that sometimes the only limit to a team's achievement is their ambition, then other teams were at the same time proving that a failure of ambition leads inevitably to a lack of achievement. If you set a high target and fall just short, there can be no disgrace. But, as Villa and Newcastle – as well as Norwich, in a slightly different way – showed, if you set a low target and fall just short, you're in trouble.

What Bilic, Barnes and many others showed is an assumption that Watford's ambition should be limited. And of course, in the end, it must be – but who are they to define its limits?

But perhaps what we learned from last season is that what matters most to a team's supporters is not, in the end, achievement at all. In terms of their final finishing position, 2015-16 was Watford's finest season for nearly three decades – since they finished ninth in 1986-87, at the end of Taylor's first spell in charge. And not only was the team successful on the pitch, but the club was apparently secure off it. Any supporter under the age of 40 would have at best only the haziest memories of experiencing anything better. So, why the long faces?

It appears possible for fans to find the well-funded pursuit of a mid-table position in the top division in some way less involving than they found the pursuit of, say, 11th in the second flight a few years earlier, with a rookie manager and a shoestring budget and a crackpot in the boardroom, or the fight to finish 13th in the same division a few years before that, while the playing squad accepted pay cuts to avoid financial Armageddon and fought their way to an FA Cup semi-final in their spare time. It could be that fans delight in the familiar, and that this particular group of fans are most of all familiar with bargain-basement teams bumbling about in the second tier in more or less heroic fashion. Or it could just be that nothing builds togetherness like adversity.

It isn't a completely outlandish idea, and it certainly seems to be what Jose Mourinho believes, to judge by his constant and wilful fomenting of discord as a means of team-building.

But if it is the latter, then that really is bad news. While the collapse of ITV Digital in 2002 suggests nothing should be taken for granted, the combination of a chunky cut of an £8.3bn TV deal and an apparently ultra-competent chairman would appear to take serious adversity out of the equation for the time being.

Everyone assumed, as Sanchez Flores departed unmourned, that Watford's fans had forgotten their team's natural place in the world. Perhaps, though, it is possible not to be too big for your boots, but simply disconcerted by how cool and shiny they are.

Simon Burnton has been writing about sport for *The Guardian* and *The Observer* since 1998. He has also written for *FourFourTwo*, *FHM*, the sadly-defunct *Arena* and anyone else who has asked nicely and paid reasonably. He once co-wrote a semi-humorous football book called *Balls!* but tries not to mention it these days.

5

At the start of 2015-16, most football pundits predicted that Watford's elevation to the Premier League would be short-lived. Plenty of Watford fans thought different.

One particular fan was especially confident. He reckoned that, from now on, Watford would be in the Premier League forever.

Olly Wicken tells the fan's story.

THE BOY WITH THE HORNET TATTOO

BY OLLY WICKEN

PART ONE

Nate pushes at the door and steps into the dimly lit studio. He sees Rose sketching at a desk. He hopes she remembers him. Be cool if she did. She's the best tattoo artist outside London.

Rose takes off her glasses. She looks up from beneath a grey-rooted mess of rock 'n' roll black hair. A smile creases her smoker's mouth.

'Hornet boy, isn't it?'

Nate beams. He feels like a minor celebrity.

'Looking after it like I told you?' she asks.

Nate shows her the work of art she inked into his forearm six months ago. The hornet has the quality of a close-up photo, with fine detail. Its head and abdomen are yellow and black, its thorax a reddish brown. Its eyes and antennae give it a look of fierce defiance. It was his best 18th birthday present by far. Everyone who's seen it has wanted one.

'Well done,' she says. 'And thanks. I've had a lot of business off the back of you showing that around. What are you after this time?'

'We got promoted at the weekend. Down in Brighton,' Nate says proudly. 'It was amazing. I want the club badge on my left pec, and Premier League badges on my arms. You know, like on an actual shirt.'

Rose looks at him for a moment. Then she puts her glasses back on and returns to her sketches. 'No,' she says simply.

'If that's too much, just the one Premier League badge, then,' Nate says.

The Prem badge is the thing he really wants. He's still giddy with promotion. He hasn't stopped tweeting about it. He can't.

Rose doesn't look up.

'Tattoos are for life,' she says. 'Watford will only be up for a season.'

Even though her studio's here on the Vicarage Road precinct, Rose strikes Nate as a typically dismissive Spurs or Arsenal fan – with no clue how brilliant the Pozzo family are at running football clubs.

'You're wrong,' he says. 'We're there to stay this time. Forever.'

Rose continues sketching.

'No, we're not,' she says.

The word 'we' jolts Nate.

'You're a fan too?'

She didn't mention this last time. But it makes sense now he remembers the love she put into the creating the hornet on his arm.

Rose pulls up a sleeve to reveal an arm almost totally inked. She points to a figure in a yellow shirt and red shorts, seemingly in mid-air, one leg stretching into the sky, with his hands down behind him. Ginger hair.

Nate thinks he half-recognises the image, but isn't sure.

'If you're a fan, you must know we're there for good,' he says.

Rose taps on the famous overhead kick.

Nate doesn't get it.

Rose takes her glasses off and looks at him.

'I'll do you the club badge. But that's your lot.'

Nate nods. It'll do for starters. He'll work on her. She'll come round.

* * *

It's sunny. Nate is in his garden.

Mum and Dad are out. He's taken off his shirt to reveal his club badge tattoo and impress the fit blonde girl who's just moved in next door.

He's also decided to display his emotional side by playing with his family's floppy-eared dog. But the girl hasn't taken the bait yet. He hears the rattle of the letter box from inside the house.

He goes in and finds an envelope on the mat. He knows what's inside. He rips it open and finds his ticket for the first match of the season.

In the top left hand corner of the ticket is a logo that says 'Barclays Premier League'.

Just below, the printed ticket details say: 'Barclays Premier League'.

So good, they named it twice.

He looks up and sees his reflection in the hallway mirror. He looks at the badge on his chest.

'You are Watford,' he tells himself.

He adds: 'You are Premier League.'

This makes him think. He stuffs the ticket in his back pocket and goes to find his shirt.

He's going back to the precinct to talk Rose round.

* * *

Nate walks into Rose's studio.

Rose is standing near her desk, hanging a small framed print of one of her tattoo designs. It's a thing of beauty. Just like the hornet on his arm.

Nate sees a page of Watford's Premier League fixtures on her computer screen. He starts to sense a bond between them. He's spent hours gazing at the fixtures too.

'I need the tattoo for the opening day at Goodison,' he says. 'Show we belong.'

For a while Rose says nothing as she hangs the print in its frame. Then she asks: 'Ever seen anyone else with a Premier League tattoo?'

'Exactly. It's a totally original idea,' Nate says.

Rose half-smiles for half a second.

'What I mean is, you never see Chelsea and Man U fans with one,' she says.

'That's what I'm saying. Not even them,' Nate says.

Rose tenses her smoker's lips.

'I did see one on a Barnsley fan recently,' she says.

'Barnsley?' Nate asks scornfully. 'Why?'

Rose rolls her eyes.

'And another on a Blackpool fan,' she adds.

Nate's face drops. Now he gets what she's saying.

'We've got the Pozzos, though,' he argues.

'That's what Blackpool fans used to say about the Oystons,' Rose replies.

Nate nearly swears at her. 'What's wrong with you?' he says. 'You've got to believe.'

He pulls his Everton ticket from his pocket. 'Look,' he says. He points to the Premier League logo. 'We're Premier League. To stay.'

Rose sighs.

'Okay,' she says. 'If you really want to commemorate our arrival in the Premier League, I'll help you.'

Nate grins. 'Brilliant,' he says. 'I knew I'd win you over.'

Rose reaches up to the framed print she's just hung on the wall. She removes the print. She hands Nate the frame.

'Perfect size for that ticket,' she says.

* * *

Rose gets back to the studio after the home win against West Ham. She switches on the shop-front sign that displays her studio's name and phone number. She's open for the evening.

She wonders how long it will be before Nate appears. He was already waiting by the door when she got back after the first home win against Swansea. She didn't let him in.

She sits down at her desk. Starts up the computer.

She sees Watford are in ninth place, nine points above the relegation zone. The sight makes her feel quite intoxicated. Today's match reminded her of watching in the mid-1980s, when Watford used to dominate established top flight teams as a matter of course. That was the Watford she grew up with. Back then, she took being in the top flight for granted.

The door opens. Nate looks in. There's a taut dog leash stretching from his hand. He looks ecstatic.

'You definitely have to do my tattoo after that,' he says. 'We were awesome.'

Rose smiles. Awesome is exactly what Watford were. Just like they used to be.

'So you'll do it now, yeah?' Nate asks.

Rose thinks for a moment. As a professional, she mustn't ink a customer with something that could become an embarrassment at a later date. As an artist, she doesn't want her work deleted in future. As a human being, she couldn't bear to inflict on Nate the blistering, infection and permanent scarring of tattoo removal.

As a Watford fan, though, she's on the verge of giving in.

She's heady with memories of the Graham Taylor years.

'I don't mean right this minute,' Nate clarifies. 'I'm just taking our dog to the vet. But next week, yeah?'

The leash in Nate's hand slackens. A short-legged brown and white floppy-eared dog waddles into the doorway.

Rose's mind is still full of memories of standing on the Vicarage Road terrace. She remembers the elation of Taylor's Watford beating the biggest clubs in the land. She gazes idly at the dog. She asks Nate what breed it is.

'Basset,' Nate says.

Rose's mind clears immediately.

Nate leaves the studio without an appointment.

* * *

On Nate's next visit, Rose is sketching again. She notices he tries starting with casual conversation this time.

'So, were you there yesterday?' he asks.

Rose looks up. She nods. She wants to come across as cool and detached, but she's not sure she's going to succeed. Since the final whistle of yesterday's 3-0 win over Liverpool she's been reading every match report she can find. She keeps staring at the league table. Watford are seventh. With almost half the season gone, they're only a point off a Champions League place.

She looks back down at her sketch. Nate peers down. He tries more casual conversation.

'What's that you're sketching?'

Rose has drawn nine black stars to form a sphere. She quickly conceals it with a magazine that's lying nearby.

'Wait, wasn't that the Champions League logo?' Nate asks.

Rose reddens.

Nate is furious.

'If you're thinking of inking Champions League badges, you can't refuse me a Premier League badge,' he says. 'Ink me now,' he demands.

Rose notices the magazine she moved is open at the page she was reading. It's an article on a new ink that makes tattoo removal easier. It's evidence she's shifted her ground.

But Nate hasn't shifted his.

'I'll have it in permanent ink, thanks,' he says. 'We're Premier League for the rest of our lives now.'

'You're being premature,' Rose says. 'We still need another 12 points to be safe.'

'Ink me now,' Nate repeats.

Rose looks at him. She pictures Odion Ighalo nodding home the third goal yesterday. It weakens her. In her mind's eye, Ighalo bears a striking resemblance to Luther Blissett.

'OK. I'll do it when we get to 40 points,' she says finally.

Nate looks surprised.

'Promise?' he asks.

Against her better judgement Rose says: 'Promise.'

* * *

Nate kneels on the pavement and raises his arms to the sky like Odion Ighalo in front of the 1881 yesterday. He's won.

He reckons his celebration would look better if he wasn't surrounded by the benches and bins of the Vicarage Road precinct. But at least, unlike Ighalo yesterday, there isn't a ridiculous six-foot furry insect kneeling alongside him.

A passer-by chants at him: 'Always believe in your soul!'

Nate chants back: 'I am Premier League, I said, I am Premier League!'

* * *

PART TWO

It's a grey Tuesday lunchtime in January. Rose is walking up the High Street. She's still in a mood after last night's abject defeat at Swansea.

She sees Nate holding hands with a blonde girl.

Rose remembers her promise to Nate after the Liverpool game. Watford haven't won since. They've lost four straight. She flushes. What had she been thinking? She'd known all along that this is what life is like in the Premier League. She should have tattooed herself a reminder before the season started. A portrait of Nordin Wooter would have done the trick.

She worries Nate will see her and hold her to her promise. A month on, he's probably even more committed to inking Premier League status into his skin – for fear of losing it.

She looks for somewhere to hide. She realises she has no choice. She ducks into the Intu centre, breaking a lifelong promise to herself that she'd never set foot in a shopping mall. She's not doing well with promises recently.

In recent years, she's told anyone who'll listen that the Premier League compromises the integrity of everyone it touches. Now it has totally destroyed hers.

* * *

Several weeks later, on the first Sunday in April, Nate picks up his girlfriend, Charlene, from next door. He walks her to a cool new café on the High Street. He hopes it'll take his mind off the abysmal 0-4 defeat he watched at Arsenal yesterday.

It felt like a match from one of Watford's previous Premier League seasons. Watford are now looking over their shoulders at a relegation scrap.

In the café, he sees Rose sitting with a coffee. Their eyes

meet. He looks away rapidly. She must think he's an idiot. He turns and queues with Charlene at the counter.

Easter has come and gone, and Watford are still short of the 40-point target. They've lost four straight – again. What had he been thinking when he said he wanted a Premier League tattoo for life? Excitement must have clouded his judgement. He reckons he had a lucky escape.

He orders two coffees and reflects that maybe he's grown up a little recently. A few weeks ago, when he first started going out with Charlene, he wanted to get her name inked onto his arm. Then he imagined asking Rose to do it. He knew exactly what Rose's reaction would be. She would have been right, too.

In fact, now he thinks about it, he reckons Rose has been good for him.

He turns and smiles at her. The only spare seats in the café are at her table. He picks up the coffees and goes over to Rose. He asks if they can join her.

* * *

Rose reluctantly allows Nate and Charlene to sit with her. She really doesn't want the same old argument about a Premier League tattoo. After yesterday, she doesn't want to discuss anything football-related.

'Rose did my tattoos,' Nate explains to Charlene.

Not a good start, Rose thinks.

'They're amazing,' Charlene tells Rose.

'Thanks,' Rose says.

Charlene asks Nate: 'Are you going to get Rose to do more?'

Here we go, Rose thinks. Since Christmas, the football has been dispiriting. She wonders if she's got the strength to keep refusing Nate his tattoo.

Nate is looking at her. He hasn't answered the question

about whether he wants more tattoos.

Rose notices she's holding her breath.

'Nothing planned,' Nate says eventually.

Rose breathes.

Nate smiles.

Rose smiles too. They're on the same wavelength at last.

Maybe she misjudged the boy.

'Actually,' she says, 'you and I may not be finished. Drop by the studio in the next couple of weeks.'

* * *

'It's amazing,' Nate says.

Watford finally reached 40 points at the weekend after Heurelho Gomes saved two penalties at West Brom.

But Nate's not talking about that.

He's looking at Rose's latest sketch for a tattoo. She's made the FA Cup shine like a mirror. Yellow and black ribbons cascade from its handles. It's beautiful.

'I've got to have that,' he says.

Before this season, he thought the FA Cup was a poor relation to the Premier League. None of the stature. But now, after Gueds smashed the second at the Emirates, and the league form fell away, he's interested.

'Only if we actually win it, of course,' he adds carefully.

He looks at Rose. In her eyes he sees something he hasn't seen before.

'I can't stop imagining it,' she says. 'I imagine us winning the cup and I actually start to tremble. I can already feel how I'll feel.'

Nate thinks Rose looks as if she might cry at any moment. He doesn't know what he'll do if she does. It feels a bit weird.

He gets out his phone. 'Can I take a photo of it?'

Rose nods. He snaps the sketch.

'It's not like we're even underdogs,' Rose says. 'Palace are in far worse form than us. After that, the final would be against someone who's no great shakes. It's a serious chance to win a trophy.'

Nate looks down at the sketch. It gleams at him.

He imagines Troy holding the FA Cup aloft. The back of his neck starts to tingle.

'I want it so badly,' Rose says. 'Our name would be engraved on that trophy for all time. Even more permanent than a tattoo.'

Nate tries saying out loud a phrase that's in his head.

'Watford, FA Cup winners, 2016.'

He likes the sound of it.

He says it again. He likes it even more.

Rose repeats it back to him. Her eyes go moist.

Rose's reaction makes Nate realise that winning the FA Cup would mean a lot more than merely avoiding relegation from the Premier League.

'No one could ever take it away from us,' he says.

Rose picks up the sketch. She holds it against Nate's arm.

'You'll be the first of my customers to have it,' Rose says.

Nate turns his head away.

Suddenly he feels foolish.

His eyes have gone moist.

* * *

Rose looks down at the deserted Wembley pitch. She slumps forward in her seat. She props her elbows on her knees. She sinks her face into her palms.

She's the only fan left in the stadium. A steward has already told her she needs to move on. That's the last thing she feels capable of doing.

She wanted to win the cup so much.

More, it seems, than anyone in yellow on the pitch.

She feels bereaved.

The steward lifts her to her feet. His impatience reminds her of Nate's impatience about getting a Premier League tattoo earlier in the season. She traipses towards the exit.

At the steps, she hears her phone ping. She stops and looks at it.

It's a picture message. She sees a sketch of a shining FA Cup with yellow and black ribbons. The message underneath says: 'Next year, eh? Nate x.'

A little of the bereavement ebbs away.

She almost smiles again.

* * *

Three weeks later, Rose lifts the needle from Nate's shoulder blade.

'Good job I didn't ask you for a Quique,' Nate says.

In the mirror he sees her smile.

'People argued he couldn't take us to the next level,' she says. 'But I think in images, and I don't know what a tattoo of the next level would look like.'

'Yes, you do,' Nate says. 'I saw a sketch on your desk, remember?'

Rose reddens again.

'Yeah, I got a bit carried away, didn't I?' she says.

Nate likes the way he and Rose can admit things to each other now.

He says: 'I was worse. I thought being a football fan was all about the level your team's at. You taught me I was wrong.'

'Did I? All I was trying to say was if you boast about how big and clever you are, it'll come back to haunt you one day.'

Nate grins. 'Chelsea have had plenty of days like that this season.'

Rose laughs.

Nate flinches as the needle goes back into his skin. To take his mind off the pain, he thinks back over the whole season. Watford's Premier League campaign was pretty good overall, but there was nothing that will live with him forever. Not like a cup win would have done. That would have meant something for all time.

He points to Rose's FA Cup design in a frame on the wall.

'Am I still first in line for that?' he asks.

He may have changed his mind about having a Premier League badge, but he knows he'll always want to hold Rose to her promise on this one.

'Definitely,' Rose answers.

Nate winces at the sting of the needle. It occurs to him that football and tattoos are the same. You want them both to have lasting meaning in your life.

This is why today's tattoo was such a good decision, he tells himself. Rose helped him decide, of course. It feels like the two of them have genuinely bonded over the course of the season.

Rose lifts the needle. The tattoo is finished.

It's small. Text only. Three words and some punctuation.

Nate looks into the mirror in front of him. He sees his shoulder blade in the magnifying mirror Rose holds up behind him.

The tattoo says: "Here's Hogg... Deeney!"

It's making his shoulder blade sting. More importantly, though, it's making the back of his neck tingle. From the instant it happened, the Leicester moment was always going to live with him forever.

Rose starts tidying up.

She says: 'It doesn't matter if it's the Premier League, the

Championship or the Southern League. Doesn't matter if it's Quique, Jokanovic or – I don't know – Colin Lee again. As fans, we want indelible moments.'

Nate looks again at Rose's FA Cup design on the wall. The moment calls for wise words – something Rose will agree with. He says: 'But we've got to be patient. Wait for the moments to come to us.'

Rose frowns. 'Steady. I haven't got as long left as you.' She sounds offended.

Nate curses himself. He should have guessed she'd take it that way. He wonders if they haven't actually bonded the way he thought.

But his doubts vanish when Rose places a gentle hand on his arm and says: 'Next year, eh?'

Olly Wicken's short fiction featured in volumes one and two of *Tales From The Vicarage*. He's also the creator and writer of Hornet Heaven – a new series of audiobook short stories about Watford FC. You can find out more at www.hornetheaven.com.

6

Kelly Somers is a lifelong Watford supporter with a seat in the lower tier of the Graham Taylor Stand.

But for the past few years, she's been largely absent because of her job in the media team at AFC Bournemouth.

In a way it meant she could not lose when Watford and Bournemouth were locked in the final-day battle for the Championship title…

And her job gave her a unique insight into what it takes for a club to adapt to the demands of the Premier League.

THE OUTSIDER ON THE INSIDE

BY KELLY SOMERS

The celebrations had finally come to an end. The changing room was empty. I stood in the tunnel at The Valley waiting for the final player to conduct his post-match media commitments. AFC Bournemouth captain Tommy Elphick emerged clutching the Championship trophy.

'Kel, can you hold this for me a second?'

Too soon.

'Erm, no Tom, I've got my hands full, just pop it on the floor.'

'No take it,' he said, and before I knew it I was holding the trophy in my arms – a bit like an awkward aunt with a baby. I didn't quite know what to do with it.

It wasn't the 'real' trophy – I knew the 'real' one was at Vicarage Road, still in its box.

'Wa-hey!' said Tom, and I knew I'd been set up. 'Let's get a picture, Kel, you're the only person from Watford that's getting their hands on that any time soon!'

To this day, the photograph of me holding the Championship trophy with black and red ribbons on has never gone further than the camera roll on my phone.

I was happy for Bournemouth – delighted for all the people who had worked so hard to win the title and promotion to the Premier League – but it was a strange feeling.

During the preceding three years, I had become accustomed to the often awkward moments that being a Watford supporter working for AFC Bournemouth brought about. I had perfected my diplomatic responses to questions about my allegiances and I had learned to deal with the bizarre rivalry that had emerged between the two sides – even when Gabriele Angella had been wrongly sent off inside two minutes of the clash between the two sides, my stance was unchanged.

But touching the trophy was different. All day, I had been convinced that Troy Deeney would be lifting it instead of Tommy Elphick and I hadn't been prepared for this.

The moment the roars erupted from the away end at The Valley, as news filtered through of Sheffield Wednesday's equalising goal, replays in my mind today.

I managed to smile and sip champagne with my friends and colleagues at Bournemouth and I was quietly toasting Watford's promotion too. It had worked out well – the two most important teams to me would both be playing in the richest and most exciting league in the world the following season.

* * *

Before I'd even put down my glass the reality of the daunting task ahead had hit me. As part of Bournemouth's media team, I knew the glare would be even more intense than during the club's promotion campaign. The huge sums of money paid to clubs by the Premier League don't just make footballers much richer than the likes of you or me, they also fund the changes the clubs must make to ensure the broadcasters who pay hundreds of millions for the rights to show matches live are able to do so.

'Section K' of the vast rulebook which arrives on the desk of Premier League club chief executives and chairmen each summer details a daunting list of broadcast requirements. There are regulations on everything from the position of television cameras to the size of the press room. For AFC Bournemouth, with an 11,300-seat stadium, finding space was more of a challenge than for most, but I'm sure it was an equally testing summer for Watford as they dealt with the expansion of the East Stand.

The redevelopment of the stand, now known as the Sir Elton John Stand, has been a long process, and the club's promotion to the Premier League would have undoubtedly changed some original architectural plans. The press box was temporarily moved to the Sir Graham Taylor Stand before completion of the Sir Elton John Stand, and when it was moved back, the club would have been forced to ensure it could seat the minimum number of journalists the Premier League rules required.

Although a potential problem, this was less of an issue than it was for AFC Bournemouth. Only a season before promotion the press box had been moved to the opposite stand but it had to be moved back because of the Premier League requirement that the press box must be on the same side of the ground as the tunnel.

Clubs are also required to provide seats for observers and overseas journalists, and there have to be camera positions in certain places, with adequate access and space for an operator, meaning lots of 'seat kills' (seats which have to be left empty) as cameras take precedence over supporters. The gantry for other cameras must also be a certain size and provide an unobstructed view – and when considering obstructions, the varying position of the sun and subsequent risk of solar glare into the camera must also be considered.

Of course all of these requirements are a big enough demand, but it also becomes a race against time to get everything finished in the short period between the initial post-season meetings and visits from Premier League officials, and the big kick-off.

I witnessed first-hand the battle AFC Bournemouth had as they repositioned the press box, turned a 3G warm-up room into broadcast rooms, and made a whole new press box – and with Watford's new stand housing press facilities, it was the same for them and their race against time went right to the line.

I heard from someone within the industry about the similar race against time happening at Vicarage Road to get everything ready for the first home game against West Bromwich Albion. But I also heard from someone at Watford that they had teams of people working through the night to get everything finished and, having been to every top flight club at least once, I can say that the blood, sweat and tears were worth it. Watford have one of the best media set-ups in the country, with a large press conference room, a room for the press to work in and an easily accessible mixed zone. (Another Premier League requirement is to have a dedicated area where journalists and broadcast rights holders can wait and where the players must pass through after the game. The players are not obliged to stop but it gives the media a chance to grab interviews.) All these facilities are in a relatively small space, making it easy for both staff and players after the match. Oh, and of equal importance, of course, the food is great!

So, with the stage set, the dramas of the summer eventually faded into the background by August 8, 2015 as the much anticipated Premier League season started. Watford were back and the Cherries were under the bright lights of the top flight for the first time. Watford gained a pleasing point on the opening day at Everton, while AFC Bournemouth were left frustrated by a disappointing defeat at home to soon-to-be-strugglers Aston Villa.

Both sides were shown very quickly how ruthless the Premier League could be, with both forced to wait until the third weekend of September before securing their first wins against

Swansea and Sunderland respectively. Having watched both sides regularly, it seemed to be that Watford, playing a style of football in stark contract to the free-flowing, somewhat nerve-racking, attacking football we had witnessed in the previous season under Slavisa Jokanovic, were the more streetwise and tighter defensively. As a result they were quicker adapting to life in the Premier League – however an early season win at West Ham for Eddie Howe's side showed glimpses of what they would go on to do more of later in the year.

* * *

Whenever Watford and AFC Bournemouth were playing on the same day, my concentration was always on my work, but whenever work prevented me being at games I always had my own reporter, with my mum providing text updates, which I would sneak a look at when I got a moment.

Everyone at AFC Bournemouth knew I was a Watford fan but my policy – and something I would advise to anyone who works for one football club but supports another – was to always remain impartial and never express an too strong an opinion about your own club, no matter how you feel. This can be difficult – I refer back to keeping quiet when Gabriele Angella was sent off on that fateful Friday night.

This included me trying not to get too carried away when Watford won because if you dish it out, you may have to take it back later on. But I was surprised by how well Watford adjusted to life in the top flight – they looked assured and, in truth, it never seemed likely they would be dragged into a relegation battle. And so, I admit, I let the odd statement about their impressive form slip to colleagues (although I was careful not to make anything sound too boastful).

So, imagine my disappointment (embarrassment, even)

when a nondescript Watford turned up on the south coast at the start of October. While attacking prowess was never something they were renowned for under Quique Sanchez Flores, that day they had to rely on a defensive slip-up, and a trend that continued throughout the season – the heroics of Heurelho Gomes – to ensure they returned home with a point.

The on-pitch action was something that won't live long in the memory but an exchange I had in the tunnel after the match will. As everything was wrapping up and I was waiting for the final few players to go through the mixed zone, Quique returned alone to the empty away changing room. Taking a quick glimpse around and being acutely aware of my surroundings and responsibilities, I let my neutral guise briefly slip. 'Excuse me Quique?' I asked.

'Yes?' he said, clocking my AFC Bournemouth-branded attire.

I mumbled something about being a lifelong Watford fan and something else about being excited about the season and thankful about how he had set the team up.

His smile widened and he was, I think, genuinely flattered. He asked me about the games I'd seen and at the end of our brief chat he thanked me, shook my hand and left to board the coach home.

Watford's Premier League journey continued its upward ascent towards the turn of the year, with form picking up throughout November before four memorable wins from five in an unbeaten December ensured they all but secured their top flight status for another season five months before the finish. For Bournemouth, it took a little longer for them to find their stride – their luckless 1-0 defeat against Newcastle summed up a frustrating period for them. However, December too saw their form pick up, with memorable back-to-back wins over Chelsea and Manchester United proving key as they gained momentum for the second half of the season.

As AFC Bournemouth were gathering pace, Watford came to a grinding, and somewhat sudden, halt. Opponents seemed to realise that by thwarting Troy Deeney and Odion Ighalo you also thwarted Watford, whereas Bournmeouth, forced to rely on different players following the disappointment of a bout of early season serious injuries, began to flourish, with wins over local rivals Southampton, fellow promoted side Norwich City and Crystal Palace. So, by the time the Hornets and the Cherries met again at the end of February, both were a comfortable distance from the relegation mire – but a previous 12 point gap between the two was ever-narrowing.

Once again, the game wasn't a classic and Watford, in particular, were less than inspiring with a clear lack of fluency and ideas when in the final third. Again, it allowed the off-pitch activity to take centre stage for me and, like last time, it was a meeting with Quique that stole the show. As ever, there were numerous talking points from the game – with a suspect looking handball by Valon Behrami from a Matt Ritchie corner the most controversial from a Cherries point of view – and it was this particular incident that caused my path to cross with Quique's again. Having completed his numerous broadcast interviews, he headed to the press room but, as he passed, the Watford press officer stopped and asked me what had been said from a Bournemouth point of view about the incident. I explained, to try and give Quique a better picture to prepare him as he headed into the lion's den of written journalists, before the Watford press officer explained who I was. He immediately remembered me, and recalled, virtually word for word, what I said to him back in October on the south coast. He left me, once again lost for words, before heading off to finish his duties within the allotted time frame.

I ensured the AFC Bournemouth players also did theirs and

then found myself in the mixed zone talking to a group of journalists, one of whom was a Watford fan. As we chatted, I felt someone tap me on the shoulder – and there he was, my little bearded Spanish friend. He bode me farewell and wished me a safe journey home before charmingly kissing me on either cheek. Having worked in a predominantly male environment throughout my whole career, I am very rarely fazed but even I admit to feeling a little flushed – and I turned to face the journalists I had been talking to and they looked exactly how I felt. That was the beauty of Quique – he knew how to play the charm offensive, and even when things weren't going his way at the end, you couldn't help but retain a soft spot for him.

That day was quickly forgotten as the Premier League juggernaut continued into the final few months of the season – and the two teams' on-pitch fortunes continued as heady form in March saw Bournemouth rapidly squeeze the gap with wins over Southampton, Newcastle and Swansea City. They, like Watford had been for many months, were on the brink of surpassing the coveted 40 points mark but both teams found it a struggle to actually get over the line.

Watford reached 40 points on April 16 – almost four months after pundits had already declared them immune from the drop – away at West Bromwich Albion, and how fitting that it was the man who had saved the team so many times already that season, Heurelho Gomes, (including in both draws over Bournemouth) who was the hero. AFC Bournemouth were due to play on the Sunday, so I was booked for a freelance announcing event the day before, and spent the afternoon battling against my dying phone battery as I rapidly refreshed Twitter for updates. Typically, it died just as West Brom got the second penalty – and unfortunately I was at an event where no one followed football. Those around me had quickly realised how much it meant to me, so a colleague checked their feed and told me Gomes had saved it again. I was convinced he must have been mistaken with the first save – but oh no, Heurelho had continued to defy the odds and saved twice from Saido Berahino. That was a happy drive home.

When Watford had got promoted before Bournemouth the previous season I was over the moon but I almost felt a sense of guilt that Bournemouth hadn't got over the line with them. I had a similar feeling this time round – Watford were safe and I wanted Bournemouth to be safe too.

Three weeks later, I was able to breathe easier again. It was a less glamorous occasion and there were no on-pitch celebrations. In fact, Bournemouth's fate was sealed by someone else. Having lost at Everton earlier in the day, we waited to see what would happen in the evening kick-off between Arsenal and Norwich. The Canaries were beaten, which made them the third team that could no longer catch the Cherries.

The full-time whistle at the Emirates blew while the plane carrying the Bournemouth team, staff, and me, was in the air on the way home from Liverpool and so the media team was able to deliver the good news. It was a momentous landmark for the club and, as we let it sink in that we'd be part of the Premier League again, I had to compose a post for the chairman's PA at home to post on social media. Oh, the glamour of working in the football media.

* * *

Mission complete – both Watford and AFC Bournemouth would again play in the Premier League in 2016-17. I could finally breathe and smile once again. Immersing yourself in football, when it's both your work and your hobby, can be exhausting and mentally draining, but the promotion-winning and survival seasons are two I have double the reason to smile about. Many club employees, like myself, say they lose their allegiance to their original club, but for me that has never been the case. I left Watford aged 18 to go to university but would always make the train journey from Loughborough back, even for midweek games which would get me back to university in the early hours. So working for another club was merely just another obstacle, but one that I would overcome.

I was born next door to the ground in Watford General Hospital and won the *Watford Observer*'s young sports journalist competition aged ten. My prize for that was to spend a day in the life of a journalist at Vicarage Road – that was the first time I realised that, although there were few places I enjoyed being as much as my season ticket seat, perhaps I could make a career out of watching football and sitting elsewhere.

Watford were the reason I fell in love with football, and gave me the basis to pursue a career I love in equal measures. My journey supporting them has been unique, but now having left AFC Bournemouth for pastures new with the Premier League's global television channel, I hope that perhaps I can occupy my beloved seat, located in the Lower Graham Taylor Stand, a little more.

Kelly Somers is a presenter currently working for the Premier League's global TV channel. Having been born next door to Vicarage Road Stadium, there was only one place her allegiances were going to lie. She has held a Watford season ticket for the majority of her life. Her unique footballing journey has also included four years working for AFC Bournemouth's press team – including during the infamous promotion-winning season.

7

If you watched Watford in the 1980s, and you were asked to pick your all-time Hornets XI, the chances are Tony Coton would be the first name on your teamsheet.

Lionel Birnie talks to the only man who has won the player of the season award three times.

Meet Watford's Number One…

WATFORD'S NUMBER ONE

BY LIONEL BIRNIE

In January 2016, Tony Coton was invited to Vicarage Road to watch two of his former teams – Watford and Manchester City – play against each other in the Premier League. The invitation was no different from many others offered to former players. 'Be our guest, have something to eat, say a few words,' he says.

As the interval approached, Coton was asked if he'd go down onto the pitch and help with the half-time draw.

'I said, "No, no, that's not my thing. I'm alright here." Richard Walker [Watford's head of communications] was trying to persuade me and eventually I said, "Oh alright then." I went down to the side of the pitch and I was looking at the fans and they were all young. I thought, "What sort of reception am I going to get here?" If you're under 30, do you remember Tony Coton playing for Watford? Probably not – maybe if you're from a family of Watford fans. I was not sure what reaction I was going to get, not just from the Watford fans but also the City fans because of going over the road,' he says, referring to his time at their deadly rivals, Manchester United.

It's not that Coton has an ego any larger than the next person, but for a former footballer the thought of stepping out onto a pitch he once graced, risking injury flinging himself at the feet of attackers, only to be met with a muted reception is not something to relish.

He needn't have worried.

Coton was greeted like a favourite son returning home and he was presented with a trophy to honour the three player of the season awards he won during his six years at Vicarage Road from 1984 to 1990. That's a record, although he does say: 'They'll be making one for Troy next because I think he'll catch me up and win four or five.'

* * *

Tony Coton is arguably the finest goalkeeper ever to play for Watford, and one of the best never to win an England cap. That's a subjective point because some great players have taken up their place between the posts at Vicarage Road. As a teenager, the great Pat Jennings began his career in England at Watford before starring for Tottenham and Arsenal in a career that spanned 20 years and two World Cups for Northern Ireland. Andy Rankin was the first recipient of Watford's player of the season award, in 1972-73, and the first of seven goalkeepers to claim the prize. Coton was the second and he was followed by David James, Kevin Miller, Alec Chamberlain, Ben Foster and, in 2015-16, Heurelho Gomes.

'It didn't go down all that well with Graham Taylor, though,' says Coton. 'He congratulated me through gritted teeth. He said: "I am genuinely pleased for you. It's why I bought you. But I don't want my defenders and goalkeeper winning player of the season because it means we're going in the wrong direction."'

While there's some merit to the manager's point of view, it could also be the case that Watford's supporters – who voted for the award – wanted to ensure that recognition was spread throughout the team. After all, the attacking players – the likes of Barnes and Blissett – enjoyed plenty of adulation for the goals they scored and the excitement they created. Coton, and defenders such as John McClelland and Wilf Rostron, who also won the award in the 1980s, did a lot of the less heralded work and perhaps the fans wanted to make sure it did not go unnoticed.

'That could be it. Whatever the reason, I appreciated it,' says Coton, although he plays down the suggestion that being popular with the fans was one of the main motivators for him. 'Anything from the supporters is nice but the way I looked at it is that when you go into professional football, the first thing you have to do is win over your team-mates. That's what I tried to do in training and in games. It's so important to have the respect of the other players for what you can do on the pitch and ultimately, if they were happy with me then I wasn't going too far wrong. I always wanted my team-mates to talk about me in the right way and I liked it if a player could say, "Oh, I played with TC at Birmingham, or Watford, or wherever, and he's a really top keeper." That's what motivated me – if I had the respect of my team-mates because of my performances then my reputation with the fans would look after itself.'

Coton is from Tamworth, which he makes clear when I incorrectly refer to him starting his professional career at his home town club Birmingham City ('Hey, I'm not a Brummie, I'm from Tamworth.') Having joined Birmingham from non-league Mile Oak Rovers 18 months earlier, the 19-year-old Coton made his First Division debut for the Blues against Sunderland between Christmas and New Year in 1980. His first touch of the ball as a professional goalkeeper was to save a penalty in the first minute. Earlier than the first minute, actually.

'Have you seen my car reg?' he asks. 'I got it on the DVLA website. It wasn't expensive, only a hundred quid or so, and it's not a flash one but it means something to me. It's TC54 PEN. It's because I saved a penalty after 54 seconds of my first match.'

As he tells the story, it becomes apparent how much

professional football has changed in the 36 years since that day. 'I wasn't told I was playing until half two,' he says. 'There were no fitness coaches, no warm-ups. In those days you ran out five minutes before kick-off and the sub fired a few shots at you and then you got on with it. I didn't realise until I got out there that the pitch was rock hard and I'd only got shorts on. I shouted to the bench to get me some [tracksuit] bottoms. I was messing about putting these bottoms on instead of warming up. I had about four touches of the ball in the warm-up and then, bang, 54 seconds in, we've given away a penalty.

'These days the coaches would give the keeper a whole load of information before kick-off about the opposition free-kick and penalty takers – "He's put the last four penalties in the bottom-right corner," that sort of thing – but I knew nothing. Sunderland's penalty taker was a guy called John Hawley but I didn't know where he put his penalties. He put the ball down, ran up and I just went full stretch at it and got it.

'Funny enough, I had a golf do at the St John's Hotel recently and it's only the second time I've ever been in that hotel – the other time was for our pre-match meal before my debut against Sunderland. I remember after the game, my dad and my brother-in-law were absolutely delighted. My dad had a massive smile on his face because of the penalty save and I said, "Dad, dad, I had a fillet steak today... For my pre-match meal." In the end, my dad said, "Will you stop going on about the fillet steak. I've never had a fillet steak, you know!" It was something special though, because braised beef slices was all we had when I was a kid!'

* * *

Coton's debut for Watford was almost as memorable, but in a very different way. He conceded five. Everton, who had beaten

Watford in the FA Cup final at Wembley four months earlier, won 5-4 at Vicarage Road.

'I expect the fans were thinking, "Who have we got here?" although I don't think I was at fault for the goals.'

The move to Watford came out of the blue for Coton. He was adjusting to life in the Second Division after Birmingham's surprise relegation the previous season. They had made a brilliant start and were top after half a dozen games. One morning, the Birmingham boss Ron Saunders – a striker who'd played for Watford in the mid-1960s, scoring 18 in 39 games – called Coton into his office. Saunders told him Watford had made an offer, which had been accepted. 'It was a shock,' says Coton. 'I wouldn't say I was keen to go, but I didn't drag my heels either. Ron explained that they didn't really want to sell but they were desperate for the money. It was a move back to the First Division and Ron spoke very highly of Graham Taylor.

'I was driven down by a guy called Norman Bodell [a Birmingham scout] and we were talking about football on the way down. I didn't really need Watford selling to me. I was a football nut then – I followed everything. I knew about them beating Kaiserslautern in Europe, I knew about them tonking Sunderland by eight. I liked the way they played – they were different, exciting. If they were on Match of the Day, I made sure I was home to watch because you knew there'd be goals and chances. I'd also played against them…'

One of those games was an FA Cup quarter-final at St Andrew's during Watford's run to Wembley the previous season, when John Barnes sent a beautiful dipping half-volley over the full-stretched Coton's head.

'I met Graham at the Ladbroke hotel off the A41 and within ten minutes I'd made up my mind. He knew all about me – he'd watched me five or six times from the terraces, he knew what I was good at, what I needed to work on, and he knew all about my family. He'd done his research and it felt like he really wanted me. I rang my dad from a payphone and he said, "Well, if you get a good feeling, go for it." I said it wasn't really just about that. I knew Birmingham were going to sell a few. I didn't want to be one of the ones left behind.'

Besides, Coton wanted to get away from the Midlands and there was one thing concerning him, particularly with Taylor's reputation for enforcing discipline.

'I'd been involved in one or two off-the-field things,' says Coton. 'Mostly it was blown out of proportion but I needed to get out of that environment.'

Coton told Taylor he had a court case hanging over him, but Taylor already knew.

'I'd been on a night out in Tamworth,' he says, picking up the story. 'I was with a mate and two friends of ours, who were girls. We were going into this place and the bouncer said to me, "You're not coming in." I said, "Why not?" "Cos I said so."

'I hadn't done anything. It's more than 30 years ago, so if I'd been drunk or a nuisance I'd tell you. Anyway, he got aggressive and put his hands on the back of my neck as I walked away. I turned round and told him to get his hands off me. We got involved a bit and I chinned him. I got a lucky break and got a couple of good ones in and he went down.

'Anyway, the bouncer didn't press charges, possibly because he was embarrassed that he was a doorman and he'd been put on his backside, but a taxi driver who was sitting in the queue opposite called the police and told them who it was – the Birmingham City goalkeeper!

'I was due to go on holiday the next day and I was all packed ready. When we got home, the police were there, so I hid in the car boot till they went. They put a note through the door saying they wanted a word but I went on my holiday for two weeks. I genuinely think that if I'd been around and had just had a chat it would have been fine and I'd have got a warning. But as it was, it got out of hand and I had to go to court.'

Step forward, Graham Taylor, character witness.

'When I told Graham the details of the case, I think he was worried he'd just spent £300,000 on a goalkeeper who wouldn't be able to play for him for a couple of months! So he got up in court like Petrocelli,' says Coton, referring to the lawyer in the 1970s American legal television show. 'He made out I was this sweet little choirboy and that since I'd signed for Watford I'd been the model of professionalism – which was true, by the way. He said the reason they signed me was to get me away from bad influences in the Midlands.

'Afterwards, my sister said she didn't recognise who Graham had been talking about in court – "That's not my brother!"'

Although Coton was found guilty, a six-month prison sentence was suspended for two years and perhaps Taylor's words proved the difference.

* * *

'When I signed for Watford, Graham said that he had a young back four. He said they were talented but they needed someone to organise them,' says Coton. Although the left-back, Wilf Rostron, was experienced, David Bardsley on the other side and Lee Sinnott in the middle were still teenagers, and Steve Terry, the other centre half, was only 21. 'Graham had Big Shirley,' says Coton, referring to his predecessor Steve Sherwood. 'He was a lovely guy, one of the nicest you could meet, and a good goalkeeper but he was a gentle giant. He wasn't the sort to really command his defence and Graham wanted me to come in and organise and give the defenders the right messages. Well, what he actually said was, "I want you to shout at them."

'Then I go and let in five on my debut!'

A couple of months later, Taylor signed John McClelland from Glasgow Rangers and that was the final part of the defensive jigsaw, so much so that Sherwood always felt that had Taylor signed McClelland first, he'd have not needed to buy Coton. Objectively speaking, that's probably not the case. Sherwood had been pilloried for his display in the FA Cup final, although unfairly because Andy Gray's goal, Everton's second, should have been ruled out for a foul on the goalkeeper.

It wasn't that Sherwood did too much wrong. He made no more mistakes than the next goalkeeper and was capable of brilliance, but Taylor wanted more from the man between the posts and felt Coton would be the ideal last line of defence.

'Manchester City fans might disagree with this,' says Coton, 'but I think that Watford supporters saw me at my very best. I think my last 30 games at Birmingham and my time at Watford were the best of my career. I loved Watford. I played more games for them than anyone else and I love going back there. It helps that I was well liked, but in terms of results, I look out for Birmingham, who I supported as a boy, and Watford, first.

'Thank God I joined Watford when I did because it was just what my career needed at that time. I've been very lucky to have an affinity for most of the managers I played for but Graham Taylor was the best and I count myself fortunate to have played for him at that time, when he was so full of energy and enthusiasm. He had a vision of how he wanted the game to be played. People thought it was long ball but if you saw us in training, you'd have seen how technical and tactical it was. People thought we played off the cuff, that we won the ball and then got it forward straight away but it was rehearsed. Those runs and those passes were planned. Everyone knew when to run, depending on who had the ball and where they had it. They knew the triggers to start off their moves. And it was so hard to play against.

'I am certain that if the technology that's around now had been around then, Graham would have embraced it and would have been at the forefront of it.

'Even then, in 1985, we'd be in the guest suite at Vicarage Road, or in a room at the training ground, watching videos of our games. With today's tech, I'm sure we'd be have been having more classroom sessions than half the schools in Watford. Graham was very analytical and he made you look at the game, how it was played and how you could get better.'

* * *

Coton was a commanding presence in the penalty area. His shouts could be heard in the often quiet air above Vicarage Road; he'd slap his defenders on the back when they made a last-ditch interception; he'd almost bellow them out of his 18-yard-box when they made a mistake. He was a fine shot-stopper too and there were more than a few games when he seemed to save Watford single-handedly, none more so than an FA Cup quarter-final at Anfield in March 1986, which ended goalless.

Not many sides went to Liverpool in those days and came away with a clean sheet but Watford did that night. Liverpool were the best side in the country and at home they penned teams in as the Kop chanted their familiar war cry, 'Attack. Attack. Attack-attack-attack.'

'It was all one-way except a couple of Barnesy efforts,' says Coton of that cup tie. 'We got battered and I got in the way of everything. I also got a bit of luck when I needed it. It's funny, though, I can't remember any particular saves, I just remember them coming at us. There's a few minutes on YouTube so I'd love a copy of the whole game if anyone has it. It must be out there somewhere. I do remember the ovation from the Liverpool fans at the end, and I remember the mum of my girlfriend at the time calling and asking if I'd seen the Daily Mirror because they'd given me ten out of ten.

'My dad also said how proud he was. Well, he was always proud of me but he was sat at home listening to it on the radio and he said that the way it sounded it was like the Alamo, with just me stood there against them.'

If the first match was a high point, the replay at Vicarage Road, on a night when the crowd rocked and swayed and twisted round the floodlight pylons and overflowed into the 'moat' between the Vicarage Road terrace and the pitch, is one that Coton replays even now, 30 years on.

'I'm still having counselling,' he says deadpan, which suggests he's only half-joking.

Watford were 1-0 up, thanks to a brilliant John Barnes free-kick, and there were just a few minutes to go when Ian Rush darted into the penalty area in pursuit of a through ball.

'Roger Milford…' says Coton, remembering the name of the referee.

Coton came out to meet Rush, went to ground and the Liverpool striker touched the ball past and then went over the keeper's body.

'I didn't touch him, that's for sure,' says Coton. 'But Rushie did what every striker would do. He toed it and there was no way he was going to reach it – it was going out of play – but he toed it past me and then went over. I still wonder now, what if I had not come for it? Should I have stayed? We'll never know, but it goes through my head.'

There was more drama at the same quarter-final stage of the FA Cup 12 months later, this time at Highbury against Arsenal and Coton ranks that as another of his finest games for Watford.

The controversy began in the run-up to the match. Coton had been sent off at Highbury earlier in the season and Taylor was furious that the authorities had decided the same referee would take charge of the FA Cup tie.

'GT did his propaganda stuff in the papers in the week before the game, complaining about the ref, so there was already an edge to the game,' says Coton. 'I made a few good saves that day but the star of the show was David Bardsley, who was playing on the wing and he absolutely roasted Kenny Sansom, who was the England left-back. He would knock it past him and leave Sansom behind and then send in a cross.

'Then there was the incident at they end, where Arsenal thought they should have had a penalty...'

Should they?

'No, I don't think so but they stopped playing. They just stopped and expected the penalty, while Luther broke down the other end and scored.'

That famous victory at Arsenal – unmatched by the Hornets for three decades – should have been followed by an FA Cup semi-final appearance for Coton. But a few weeks before the semi-final against Tottenham Hotspur Coton got injured.

'We were just finishing training and Steve Harrison [the coach] said, "Let's do a bit of finishing." I can still see it now. Luther hits it and it was straight at me. I put my hand out and it got me right on the thumb. I felt it straight away so I took my glove off. I was hoping to see a dislocation because you can pop that back in, happens all the time, but it wasn't out of the joint. Then it started to swell up and I knew it wasn't right.

'I said, "I think I've broken me thumb," and everyone just looked at me and said, "Oh, don't say that."

'We packed it in ice and I went to the hospital for an X-ray. It was broken. They told me I had no chance of the semi-final, or the final if we made it. I remember getting back to the ground and the players were all looking out, hoping I'd be there with a smile to say, "It's alright lads." I cried. Big tough Tony

Coton in tears because I knew I'd miss the semi-final.'

In the days leading up to the semi-final, Coton's understudy Steve Sherwood got injured too and that led to the extraordinary call to Gary Plumley, a former Newport County goalkeeper who was running a wine bar in Wales. He was also the son of Watford's chief executive Eddie Plumley who had been running a wine bar in Wales, to join Watford at their training base at Lilleshall. The story is documented in full in Enjoy the Game but Coton still believes it is Graham Taylor's biggest mistake in football. 'Well, that and letting the cameras in for that Do I Not Like That documentary when he was England manager,' he says.

'I still believe a half-fit Shirley [Steve Sherwood] was a better bet than an amateur goalkeeper who'd been running a wine bar.'

Tottenham started the game at a high tempo, determined to test Plumley from distance right from the off and they were 3-0 up in no time. It ended 4-1.

'Every team would do that if they thought the keeper was suspect,' says Coton. 'But it wasn't the real problem. The problem was it knocked the confidence in the rest of the team. They'd have been more confident with Shirley – or even a young David James out of the youth team. Graham said he wanted to protect Shirley, that he didn't think it was fair to expose him, half-fit, in a high profile game, but Steve wanted to play. He saw it as his chance to perform and put the [1984] FA Cup final behind him.

'That was a horrible day – and not just because it was at Villa Park! I didn't want to go. In my six years at Watford I never had a single negative reaction from a Watford supporter except that day. I was walking along the touchline before the start of the second half, my arm in plaster, when a fan came running down the steps and said, "Oi, Coton, it's your fault we're losing this."

I went to get involved and GT pulled me away. I suppose it was a back-handed compliment in a way, but that was a terrible day because I wanted to be out there.'

* * *

Graham Taylor left at the end of that season and Dave Bassett came in. The new manager's relationship with Coton was not always the best and around Christmas time, with poor results stacking up and relegation looking increasingly likely, the goalkeeper found himself one of the scapegoats when he was dropped in favour of Mel Rees. It was a decision that almost caused a mutiny in the Watford dressing room and within a month, Bassett was gone, replaced by former coach Steve Harrison.

Harrison could not save Watford from the drop and it will perhaps surprise supporters who do not remember that era that a player of Coton's calibre stuck around for another two seasons. These days, there'd be a fast-track back to the top flight.

'Tottenham tried to get me,' says Coton, 'and I was going to go but Steve begged me to stay and the club offered me a six-year contract. The money wasn't great but it would have taken me up to ten years and Elton said he'd do a concert for my testimonial. I thought that would be a few bob – 27,000 people packed into Vicarage Road to see Elton John. Harry [Steve Harrison] did a good job of persuading me but after we failed to get promoted, he went and Colin Lee came in.'

Lee brought in a former Celtic manager, David Hay, as one of his coaches and he showed his lack of familiarity with the English game one day during the summer.

'We were training two days a week all summer, except for a two-week holiday,' says Coton. 'I'd talked to Manchester City and the clubs had agreed a deal and one day I went in and said,

"I'm off then…" David Hay said, "Off? Where are you off to?" "I'm going to Man City." "Oh, really? Who are you then?"

'I thought, well, it's time I was moving on if the coach doesn't know who I am! Mind you, a few years later, the first time I met Alan Ball at City he called me Andy Dibble. I said, "No, gaffer, that's Andy Dibble over there."'

* * *

In the summer of 1990, after six seasons, almost 300 first-team appearances and three player of the season awards, Coton moved on to Manchester City for £1million.

At Maine Road, he won another couple of player of the season awards and, with his former Watford manager Graham Taylor now in charge of the national team, might have expected an international cap.

However, Coton believes his international chances were scuppered by his brush with the law in 1984. He's been told that Bobby Robson wanted to call Coton up in the mid-1980s, when he was undoubtedly one of the best goalkeepers in the country and at the peak of his powers, but the FA bigwigs blocked it.

'I don't know…' Coton says. 'I didn't really buy that. When GT came in, I thought I might get a cap. I went on a tour to Australia, I went to San Marino, I went to Russia. Eventually I got the second half of a 'B' game against France at Loftus Road and he [Taylor] said, "Look, that's as far as it'll go. I'm not allowed to pick you. That was it, that was my England career.

'I don't know. Tony Adams and Paul Merson were getting picked at the time and they had trouble off the pitch. Adams had been to prison so it's not consistent. I'd rather he'd said, "I don't fancy you."'

* * *

After Manchester City, Coton moved to Sunderland. In the years since leaving Vicarage Road, he'd never had an opportunity to return because City and Watford were in different divisions. 'Every time there was a cup draw I hoped to get Watford away,' he says. 'It was one of the things I wanted – to go back to Vicarage Road, not because I thought I'd get this great reception or anything but because I wanted to say thanks.'

Then, in 1996, the balls were kind and Watford were drawn to play Sunderland in an early round of the League Cup. 'As soon as the draw was made, I went in to see Peter Reid [Sunderland manager]. I said, "You're not thinking of changing the team round for the League Cup are you? Because I have to play in that one."'

The first leg was at Vicarage Road and Coton stepped into the ground for the first time in six years to find it considerably different. 'Two of the stands were the same – the Rous Stand was built in my time and the old stand on the other side was still the same, but they'd put up two new stands at the Vicarage Road end and the Rookery.

'I remember when I ran up to the goal at the home end, the reception I got will stay with me for ever. As I got into my six-yard box a fan jumped over the wall and I thought, "What's this?" He stretched his hand out and said, "I just want to thank you for all your displays when you were here and I want to shake your hand."

'When I went back to Vicarage Road for the Manchester City game I was really impressed with the atmosphere. The ground now is terrific with the flags and all the songs. Every player's got a song now, haven't they. Back in my day, they might have sung "England's Number One," if I made a good save. Or they used to sing, "Tony, Tony; Tony, Tony,"' he says, recalling the old chant that used to sound like the pealing of church bells.

During his time coaching at Manchester United, Coton has watched the art of goalkeeping change although, he says, 'It's still basically the same. You have to organise your defence and keep the ball out, but there are trends and fashions. There are a lot of foreign goalkeepers in the Premier League and they are coached differently, from a young age. They knock it, they parry it. Sometimes I watch a keeper and I cringe. I think, "Why punch that when you can catch it?" But it's what the goalkeeper is trained to do, what he's comfortable with. The worst thing for a keeper is trying to do something that's not natural to you.'

Coton was in charge of goalkeeper recruitment at Aston Villa when we spoke, although he was quick to point out that the Italian Pierluigi Gollini was not one of his recommendations. 'He was at [Manchester] United and he couldn't get in the [under] 16s. He's not for me, and I didn't want the Villa fans thinking he was one of mine because they'd say, "Hang on, the Birmingham City man is trying to stitch us up here!"'

He says that, when he watches a goalkeeper, he's careful not to judge them by the style of play that was prevalent when he was one of the country's top players.

'It doesn't matter what I'd do in a certain situation. I can't criticise a keeper for punching something that I'd prefer to catch. If he prefers to punch, that's fine, but does he punch well, does he punch it into safe areas? I used to pride myself on holding everything. If it was a long range shot, I'd want to hold it with soft hands, rather than put it round the post because what's a corner? A corner's pressure. The keepers today will tell you the ball is different, that it moves, that it's harder, and maybe it is.

'It's the same as playing out from the back – the sweeper-keeper. Everyone gets carried away about it but if a manager wants to play that way, that's his right. I just think there are times to play and times to just stick your boot behind it and get the ball away, allow your defenders to get out and ease the pressure.'

And that brings us to Heurelho Gomes, winner of Watford's player of the season award during the 2015-16 Premier League campaign, the first time the Hornets have survived in the top flight since Coton's days.

'I knew Gomes when he was in Holland [playing for PSV Eindhoven]. I watched him over there a few times and thought he was a good keeper. He makes great saves and he comes and gets things. He makes mistakes but show me any goalkeeper – any player – who doesn't. A goalkeeper makes a mistake and it can be more costly. I've always rated him because he works well with his defence. It's just a shame he's 35 and not 28 because that's the only thing against him.'

* * *

Coton's three player of the season awards earned him a place in Watford's hall of fame. He was inducted second, after Luther Blissett.

'I work with Tommy Mooney at Villa and you know Tommy, he loves talking about his career! When we first worked together we were in the office talking about our careers. We'd both played for Watford, both played for Birmingham, now we're at Villa, so we had a fair bit in common. We were talking about people we knew and all that. But he didn't know my full background.

'One of the lads in the office was asking Tommy about Watford and Tommy was sitting back in his chair giving it all this, "Oh yeah, I was fourth into the hall of fame."

'Quietly, I said to the lad, "Ask me next…" so he said, "Are you not in the hall of fame at Watford, Tone?"

'Tommy looked straight up and said, "You're not in it are

you? Are you? What number?"

'Number two, I said.

'He looked gutted that I beat him into the hall of fame and now, whenever we speak on the phone it's, "Hello, is that four? It's two here."'

Tony Coton, number two? It doesn't sound quite right. For Hornets fans of a certain vintage, Tony Coton will always be Watford's Number One.

8

Promotion to the Premier League gave radio commentator **John Anderson** more opportunities to cover his team — but that wasn't always a good thing.

It meant having to keep his emotions under control in the commentary box or studio booth whenever he was describing a Watford match.

And sometimes that was easier said than done.

BRINGING WATFORD TO THE WORLD

JOHN ANDERSON

Like all Watford fans, that YouTube clip of the players celebrating promotion to the Premier League on the coach back from Brighton at the end of the 2014-15 season is etched very vividly upon my memory. Rarely can a late equaliser at Rotherham have featured so prominently in the club's history and I've often wondered whether goal scorer Jordan Bowery considered heading down to Watford after their game against Norwich, knowing he wouldn't have had to buy a drink all night.

The end of the club's eight-year hiatus from the top flight prompted my wife and I to buy his 'n' hers matching season tickets in the Sir Elton John stand and I resolved to improve my pitiful attendance record at The Vic. In the end I made five visits during the season for the league games against West Brom, Manchester United, Norwich, Chelsea and the third round FA Cup tie against Newcastle. I also went to the semi-final at Wembley but the less said about that the better.

As well as the obvious elation as a fan, I also had a professional reason to celebrate the club's success. A return to the top flight meant I would have the chance to commentate on Watford's games on a more regular basis. While we were a Football League club this had only been a rare occurrence, such as the Boxing Day 2014 defeat at home to Wolves when I was providing commentary for the world TV feed.

For the past four years I have been working as a freelancer for TalkSport Live who are the Premier League's global broadcast partner for radio and provide commentaries on all 380 matches each season to a worldwide audience outside the UK and Ireland, not just in English but also in Spanish, Arabic and Mandarin. Because of the financial and logistical constraints of such an enormous undertaking, the vast majority of matches are covered 'off tube'; that is to say we are commentating in front of television monitors at TalkSport's rapidly expanding headquarters a short walk from London's Waterloo Station.

My first opportunity to commentate on Watford came in late September with the visit of Crystal Palace in one of those contractual obligation televised Sunday lunchtime games that is probably regarded by most neutrals as somewhat less tempting than a plate of roast beef and Yorkshire pudding. Nevertheless, the game came off the back of two encouraging wins against Swansea and Newcastle and I was hoping, impartially and professionally of course, to be bringing news of a hat trick of victories to our listeners in 69 countries across the world.

I also had the pleasure of sharing commentating duties with former Palace defender Matt Lawrence who, prior to his stint at Selhurst Park, had captained Millwall in the 2004 FA Cup final. He partnered former Hornet Darren Ward in central defence against Manchester United in Cardiff that year but sadly they weren't quite up to the task of shackling the might of Cristiano Ronaldo, Ryan Giggs, Paul Scholes and Ruud van Nistelrooy and lost 3-0. Matt is unique among footballers in that he has a degree in American literature from a university in upstate New York and counts the Velvet Underground and Primal Scream among his favourite bands.

Sadly there wasn't much for us to scream about as the match rather depressingly mirrored the previous meeting between the sides when Watford surrendered meekly at Wembley in the 2013 Championship play-off final and once again we lost to a single penalty in an utterly forgettable encounter.

Thankfully my next Watford commentary was to be rather more uplifting. As soon as the fixtures for the new season were released in the summer, it was obvious that the Christmas period would be absolutely crucial to the club's survival hopes. I can only assume that the person who inputs the data to draw up the schedule was a Luton fan who had spent that morning gridlocked on the ring road outside the shopping centre and decided upon a particularly sadistic form of vengeance; Liverpool, Chelsea, Tottenham and Manchester City all in the space of 13 days. There was a flaw in their evil plan though. The three games which preceded that sequence were winnable ones against Aston Villa, Norwich and Sunderland and, with Odion Ighalo in unstoppable form, nine points were duly accrued.

And so it was that I had the pleasure and privilege of commentating on a game which has entered the club's folklore as the Golden Boys entertained Liverpool who, under new boss Jürgen Klopp, had recently achieved superb wins at both Chelsea and Manchester City.

Commentating from a TV screen presents very different challenges to doing so from a prime position at the ground. Effectively you are relying on what pictures the programme director decides to use. For example, if you are unsure about the identity of a goal scorer, then a quick cut to a close-up shot of a celebrating manager or the cheering crowd doesn't help very much. Typically, the player who's just scored may be buried underneath a pile of jubilant team-mates by the time the director has gone back to the scene on the pitch and you have to wait until the players have all got up before revealing the scorer. Another problem often arises when a goal is disallowed by an offside flag which is out of shot. You may spend several seconds describing the goal and pulling out stats about the scorer and the team, only for the screen to eventually reveal the assistant referee with his arm aloft, forcing a hasty backtrack.

With this in mind, a very early goal scrambled into the net in a crowded goalmouth following an inswinging corner is not the easiest thing to deal with. Fortunately when it's your own team involved, player identification is less of an issue and in this instance I was confidently able to spot that Nathan Aké had got the vital touch after Liverpool keeper Adam Bogdan delighted us with his impression of a man in a blindfold trying to catch a bar of soap.

Another advantage of being a fan is that you are likely to devour information about Watford more keenly than, for example, Swansea or Bournemouth. As a result you have a mental reservoir of material to draw on to fill the gaps in the action. With 15 minutes gone and Aké the key figure so far, I was recalling an interview I'd read with the on-loan Chelsea left-back when I was caught on the hop and forced into an about-turn mid-sentence as a Troy Deeney long ball flew forward...

'He's a very articulate young man, there was a very good newspaper article about him...but let's not worry about that at the moment because Ighalo's got the better of Skrtel...and he's found the net...Odion Ighalo doubles Watford's lead!!!!!'

By this time I was delivering the words from an upright position with both fists clenched, pumping my arms in the air in joyous celebration.

The third goal, five minutes from time, was a commentator's dream. A crisp, clear, decisive move, a pinpoint cross and then a close range header to provide the final act of the drama, offering me the opportunity to tie up all the loose strands of the story perfectly...

'Here's Odion Ighalo for Watford...finds Deeney...Deeney crossfield to Valon Behrami...and it's headed in by Ighalo... Watford have sealed the deal...five minutes from the end he's done it again...Ighalo with the simplest of headers....it's a dozen goals this season for him...and Watford, who were beaten 3-0 by Liverpool the last time the two teams played here, are now 3-0 up against Liverpool…and have three points against Liverpool.'

My co-commentator on this occasion was Chris Iwelumo whose Watford career, by his own admission, never threatened to approach the heights scaled by Ighalo's but who retains a strong affinity for the club. He declared it to be the finest Hornets performance he'd ever witnessed and few would argue. But while we were thrilled to be able to describe such an epic display, there was a tinge of personal disappointment not to have actually been at The Vic on one of those days that will live with the fans forever.

On the other hand I was secretly rather pleased to be ensconced in a warm studio on a Wednesday night in early March having negotiated the Victoria and Bakerloo lines rather than the M1-M6 corridor for a fixture which Watford had lost ten times consecutively. The last time we beat Manchester United in any competition came on another midweek evening nearly 30 years previously when an 18-year-old Iwan Roberts, another ex-Hornet with whom I have enjoyed working enormously at TalkSport Live, announced himself to the world with the winning goal.

Given that this fixture at Old Trafford came during a sequence of just one win in ten Premier League matches since the Liverpool game, there was little cause for optimism. But in truth it wasn't that dissimilar a performance on a frustrating night of what ifs. What if Ighalo had been a little more clinical in front of goal? What if he had spotted Deeney to his left instead of choosing to shoot in the first half? What if David De Gea hadn't been in such incredible form? What if Matteo Darmian's blatant shirt pull on Sebastian Prödl had been spotted? But it can be a cruel game as we all know and, in the end, Juan Mata's late free kick rendered all of that academic.

In their different ways the two matches had offered me the opportunity to cast off the shackles of impartiality without appearing biased. With the Liverpool win I could justifiably eulogise about a Watford victory and its potential significance within the club's aim of Premier League survival, while the manner of the defeat at United allowed me to express the not unreasonable sentiment that the better team had lost.

Normally commentators are given a few weeks' notice as to which game we will be covering on any given weekend and my last assignment of the season was meant to be a final Sunday nail-biter as Sunderland came to Vicarage Road. But four days earlier the Black Cats had beaten Everton at the Stadium of Light and in doing so ended the relegation battle as the win kept them safe and sent arch rivals Newcastle and also Norwich down to the Championship.

It is never easy to commentate on games in which there is nothing at stake and, while low on genuine quality, this one proved entertaining enough to make it a relatively enjoyable experience. The backdrop, of course, had been the confirmation on the Friday that Quique Sanchez Flores would be leading Watford for the final time as head coach. This news appeared to have split our supporters into two factions: those who considered this to be a dreadfully unkind fate to befall a man who had preserved our Premier League status and led us to an FA Cup semi-final; and others who felt he had taken the club as far as he could and that the poor recent results and performances demanded a fresh approach.

I unashamedly admit that I was very much in the first camp and so, it seemed, were most of my media colleagues whether they were Watford supporters or not. However, I can fully understand why many fans who, unlike me, had been to a majority of the games were beginning to feel unhappy. Such an example was my own wife who attended 16 matches at The Vic and would, more often than not, return home bemoaning the paucity of quality and entertainment value on show.

Before I leave the 2015-16 season behind, I can reveal that the most enjoyable time I spent in the studio was on a day when I wasn't even covering the Hornets. On Sunday, March 13, I was commentating on doomed Aston Villa against title-chasing Tottenham Hotspur in a four o'clock kick off at Villa Park for which our build-up and preview would begin at 3.30pm.

Obviously there was a far more important fixture taking place earlier that afternoon at the Emirates and, rather than miss any of the action from our FA Cup quarter-final against Arsenal, I made sure I arrived in plenty of time to watch the game. My fellow commentator and Watford fan Toby Gilles, who was in the building to do a news reading shift, had the same idea and had also turned up early, resplendent in a vintage Hornets replica shirt. The working area at TalkSport is in the basement of the four-storey building and comprises an open-plan production area with a row of booths running along one side from which we do our commentaries. Because there were only a few games that afternoon, many of these were vacant and Toby and I took up residence in two adjacent ones to watch a feed of the game.

By a quirk of fate there was a third Watford supporter on duty that day. Jamie Dickens, a 21-year-old City University journalism student, was gaining valuable work experience as an intern under the aegis of TalkSport Live's wonderfully extrovert editor Tom Rennie and his venerable producer Matt Gubbins. This was a massive day for Jamie quite apart from our FA Cup game; he was undergoing a trial shift which would go a long way toward determining whether he would make the step up to being hired as a freelance producer for the following season.

As the game got underway, every now and then an ooh or an ahhh, a cry of anguish or a gasp of relief, would emanate from

Toby and myself but we did our best to keep the volume down, mindful that the noise might bleed into the booth where the commentary of the game was taking place a few feet away. But five minutes into the second half, when Ighalo spun away from Gabriel and shot low into the bottom corner, we could contain ourselves no longer. We both turned out of our booths and leapt into each other's arms, whereupon Toby, who is younger and fitter than I am, proceeded to hurl me up into the air and catch me three or four times before depositing me back on terra firma.

Strangely, given the quality of the goal, we were more restrained when Adlène Guedioura's thunderbolt hit the roof of the net 13 minutes later, possibly due to the sheer disbelief of both witnessing such a magnificent instinctive strike and of realising that a win which would take us to Wembley was now on the cards. The rest of the game was watched, as it was by everyone, through splayed fingers with fluttering hearts and the kind of wrenching in the gut that is almost unique to occasions such as these. This reached its apotheosis with Danny Welbeck's late miss which my friend and fellow commentator Jonathan Pearce summed up so brilliantly on that night's *Match Of The Day...*

'Wide! Impossibly wide!!'

At the end Toby and I embraced each other in a rather more restrained manner, the overriding emotion being relief rather than elation. Alas, poor Jamie was unable to take part in the celebrations as he had spent the entire match hunched over a computer in a state of total concentration as he sought to demonstrate that he was up to the complicated task of compiling and editing the highlights packages and other non-live elements of the broadcast quickly and efficiently. His job was no doubt made harder by the antics of two buffoons, displaying a distinct lack of studio etiquette, pogoing around behind him. At one point Toby even gently berated him for his lack of enthusiasm when our first goal was scored and, to his credit, Jamie did allow himself a punch of the fist when Guedioura's goal went in.

Within minutes of the final whistle at the Emirates I had to try to compose myself and take up my position alongside the far more calm and collected figure of former Spurs midfielder Kevin Watson to start the coverage of the Villa v Spurs game. I can honestly say that, after the drama of the previous couple of hours, I wasn't completely focused on Mauricio Pochettino's bid to maintain Tottenham's title challenge with another win. I can't remember anything at all about the game other than two Harry Kane goals either side of half-time which secured a routine win against arguably the worst side in Premier League history. However, I do recall taking great pleasure in regularly informing our listeners that, in case they had missed it earlier, Watford had stunned holders Arsenal in the FA Cup and were heading to Wembley.

The postscript to all of this is that Toby woke up the next morning with an excruciating pain in his lower back and could barely get out of bed. It seems the folly of flinging a 13 stone football commentator up and down in celebration had taken its toll. The agony stayed with him all week and in the end he had to fork out £200 on four osteopathic sessions to put the damage right.

He later told me, as I proffered an apology, that it had all been worthwhile. And I'm delighted to say that, despite our unintentional efforts to put him off, Jamie passed the audition.

John Anderson is a freelance sports broadcaster and commentator who has covered multiple World Cups, European Championships and Olympic Games in a career spanning more than 30 years. He is also the author of a humorous memoir *A Great Face for Radio.* You can follow him on Twitter @GreatFaceRadio.

9

Sometimes **John Anderson** has to follow Watford's fortunes from afar, tuning into commentary while he's away on an assignment.

Last autumn, as Odion Ighalo scored twice to beat West Ham, he found himself in the Atacama Desert in Chile.

And what he saw there told him all he needed to know about how Watford's season was going to turn out.

FLOWERS IN THE DESERT

BY JOHN ANDERSON

Every seven or eight years or so, something rather magical occurs in Chile's Atacama Desert. When the levels of rainfall produced by the storm known as El Niño are especially high, the harsh terrain of the world's driest habitat becomes transformed by a pink and purple carpet of flowers which bring this most inhospitable corners of the Earth vividly to life.

Those of you who read my chapter in the first *Tales from the Vicarage* book will know that my job as a football reporter and commentator often deprives me of the opportunity to witness some of Watford's most memorable matches first-hand. So it was that in the late October of our first season in the Premier League since 2006-07 I found myself gazing in wonderment at the Atacama Desert's miracle of nature while enjoying a day off from covering the FIFA Under-17 World Cup in Chile. This junior tournament roughly follows the format of the World Cup itself, even down to the fact that England arrived in South America with high hopes but were absolute rubbish and went out at the group stage without winning a game.

Even by the standards of previous Atacama Desert flower shows, 2015 had produced an especially spectacular display. El Niño had been relentless in March bringing floods to a region which normally experiences less than an inch of rainfall a year and producing a technicolour tapestry, the breadth and intensity of which hadn't been witnessed in this area of greys and browns for nearly two decades.

During my fortuitous visit to this scene of splendour I felt my mobile phone vibrate in my pocket. A glance at the screen revealed via my Watford FC text feed that a goal from Odion Ighalo had put us ahead against West Ham. My cry of triumph punctuated the stillness and serenity of the scene and I instinctively began to hum *Gold* by Spandau Ballet to the bewilderment of my fellow tourists. A mere half an hour or so later I treated them to another chorus as news of Iggy's second goal reached the Lower Andes branch of the Hornets Fan Club.

In the midst of these glad tidings and the extraordinary natural scenery all around me, I pondered the cyclical nature of things and it occurred to me that, in the Premier League era, our club's fortunes have followed a similar path. Seemingly endless periods of barren, featureless conformity punctuated by short-lived bursts of regeneration and colour. This year though, there was a sense that something extra special was blossoming, that this time it might be more spectacular than ever before.

The West Ham win was, of course, a second successive victory following an equally good performance at Stoke the previous weekend. I had followed that game from my Chilean base in the city of La Serena via the magnificent service provided by TalkSport Live.

Just a few miles down the Pacific coast from La Serena is the port of Coquimbo which had been hit by a huge earthquake and subsequent tsunami just a month earlier, causing massive destruction to the seafront area. Although quakes are commonplace in the area, they rarely strike with such force and a stroll along the beach revealed boats that had been tossed up onto the sand, huge tracts of destroyed paving, uprooted lamp posts and the twisted wreckage of children's play areas.

Every now and then you would experience a much more minor tremor in which an unsettling four of five seconds of vibration would pass through your body. It was a bit like feeling a spot of heavy aeroplane turbulence while sitting at breakfast or lying in bed. I'm sure the people in the room next door to mine might have been mistaken for thinking another had struck as I leapt up and down in celebration of Troy Deeney's wait for a first Premier league goal finally coming to an end at the Britannia Stadium.

Of course the season continued to blossom for a while, reaching its apex with the pre-Christmas win over Liverpool, but, like the desert plains, the purple patch was followed by a barren spell as the turn of the year saw the performances wane, the entertainment subside and (the FA Cup quarter final at Arsenal aside) the results worsen.

But with Leicester winning the title and Watford achieving Premier League survival in relative comfort, the 2015-16 season has shown us that moments of miracle and wonder can exist in even the harshest and most challenging of landscapes. I will always associate the campaign with that Saturday when I stood 7,000 miles away from Vicarage Road staring in awe at the flowers of Atacama.

And the irony didn't escape me that in Spanish, the national language of Chile, the word for flowers is *flores*.

10

David Harrison explains why Lloyd Doyley is much more than just a long-serving defender.

Doyley played for the Hornets during good times and bad, always giving everything he had to the cause, even if there were more gifted players around him.

But now Doyley has gone, his place in the history books means that it's clear he represents a vital link between Old Watford and New Watford.

LIFE WITHOUT LLOYD

BY DAVID HARRISON

'There'll never be another like him'
'A proper Watford defensive legend'
'They broke the mould'
'The ultimate one-club man'

These were sentiments expressed on and around Sunday, April 21 2002, when Nigel Gibbs made his final Watford appearance, as a substitute in a surprisingly lively 3-2 Vicarage Road defeat at the hands of Gillingham. You'll remember the game – it marked our joyous release from Gianluca Vialli's ludicrous reign but also featured a stunning goal from what at that time appeared the compelling, emergent talent of Anthony McNamee.

·Elsewhere on the pitch it would be fair to say few among the impressive 15,674 crowd were particularly interested in the gawky, ungainly teenager making just his fifth Vicarage Road start. And yet Lloyd Doyley would, over the next two decades, take his place alongside Gibbsy and just a handful of others in the Hornet record books.

There must be something about the right-back position. I've been around for a while and in my time three specialists in the role – Duncan Welbourne, Nigel Gibbs and Lloyd Doyley – have appeared in getting on for half of Watford's games. It's an extraordinary demonstration of both loyalty and longevity, especially as almost ten years elapsed between Welbourne's departure in 1974 and Gibbsy's arrival on the scene.

Welbourne, Gibbs and Doyley have plenty in common. They are not chest-beating, crowd-rousing, heroic defensive figures like Robbo, or Jay Jay Jay from the USA, or even Danny Shittu, they are solid citizens outwardly unaffected by public acclaim, quietly getting on with the job in hand. Rarely excessively brilliant, nor especially poor. Professionals admired by fellow professionals.

It's not my role to argue the relative playing merits of the three. However I would suggest Doyley's achievement represents the most remarkable demonstration of loyalty, in that when Welbourne and, to a degree, even Gibbs, were plying their trade, the one-club man was not especially unusual, with the awarding of ten-year testimonials commonplace. Not these days.

This chapter was never intended as a statistical assessment of Lloyd's time at The Vic, much more a series of personal recollections, but it would be wrong not to outline the chronology of his achievements.

Lloyd made his Watford debut, as a substitute under the Vicarage Road lights, against Birmingham City in September 2001. The game finished 3-3 (Cox, Glass and Smith) but was memorable not for any of the six goals, rather the spectacular departure from the arena of Pierre Issa. Vialli's lumbering South African centre-half fell uncomfortably onto his shoulder in front of the Rookery, at which point his problems were just beginning.

A stretcher party, including some members of one of the club's junior teams, at least one of whom was subsequently reported to have been wearing slippery, leather-soled shoes, scooped up the stricken defender only to swiftly catapult him straight back onto the rain-soaked turf, landing once again on the damaged shoulder. I'd like to say we heard the resultant yelp of pain 20 rows back in the Rookery, but my memory could be playing tricks.

Suffice to say, as a consequence of this slapstick interlude, together with the subsequent appearance of Tommy Mooney as a Blues half-time substitute, the identity of Issa's replacement passed with little comment. It provided, however, a first Vicarage Road glimpse of none other than Lloyd Colin Doyley.

Doyley fitted into a three-man defensive line alongside Robbo and Ramon Vega. His appearance led Matt Rowson to observe, in his *Blind Stupid and Desperate* match report: 'Doyley, with his excitable demeanour, long throw and attacking instincts needs only the propensity to make a bee-line for goal whenever he gains possession to be the spit of Ben Iroha. His often vital support to the attacking play was tempered with a defensive nervousness which gifted some openings to City.'

Fair to say those natural attacking instincts were subsequently sacrificed, to some extent at least, in pursuit of the defensive excellence with which we were all to become increasingly familiar.

Lloyd's debut as a substitute was immediately followed by a first start, in a 1-1 draw against Preston at Vicarage Road. He was far from a permanent fixture in Vialli's side but when funny stuff was happening, he generally seemed to be not far away. He started in a game against Stockport when Robbo, the only defender in the penalty area, somehow blasted a ridiculous own goal past a bewildered Uncle Alec. Then, later the same month in a League Cup tie against Charlton, Lloyd was out there when the same man unforgettably scored from a tackle, in front of the Rookery. Although only a bit-part player and still just a teenager, Lloyd was quickly becoming a proper part of Vicarage Road life.

Vialli departed, with the club in a hideous financial state (the two facts being not entirely unconnected) and the altogether more suitable Ray Lewington assumed control but it was Aidy's arrival, late in the 2004-05 season, which saw Lloyd's fortunes take a sharp turn for the better.

He was a regular in the fantastic 2005-06 season which began with a ghastly home defeat to Preston but ended, unforgettably, with that thumping 3-0 win over Leeds United. 'Doyley, Mackay, Demerit, Stewart' was the back-line at both Selhurst and Cardiff in those wonderful play-off games. I can still see Doyley pinging passes down the line in front of the Rous Stand that season for Ashley Young to run on and hurdle some clumsy full-back before putting Marlon King through on the Rookery goal.

We won't linger on the horrible Premier League season which followed, suffice to say that Lloyd made 17 top-flight starts as relegation was painfully inevitable from early in the season. I have a vivid recollection of one particularly gruesome afternoon at The Valley when Aidy decided to play the percentage game and look to painstakingly develop possession, seemingly on an NFL-inspired basis. The plan, such as it was, comprised Lloyd taking a series of right-wing throw-ins, each intended to gain a couple of yards. The whole sorry season was hard to watch.

Lloyd remained generally a regular as we settled back into life in the Championship, although he did lose his place briefly to Lee Bromby, he of the prodigious long throw. The first season after relegation wasn't too bad, ending with that play-off defeat to Hull City, but Aidy's days were numbered and he finally departed after DeMerit lost his head in a ridiculous 4-3 home defeat to Blackpool.

Brendan Rodgers joined for a brief spell late in 2008, during which the 'Lloydinho' tag, which endured for the rest of his time at the club, was conceived by the manager after Lloyd played Priskin in on goal with the most sumptuous pass, struck with the outside of his foot.

Lloyd's disciplinary record has always been good but he excelled himself that season, playing over 40 games and waiting until the last of those before collecting his first booking, at home to Derby. Eustace scored for the visitors that day and was no doubt responsible for winding Lloydy up!

Despite many years of stalwart defensive service, Lloyd will of course be best remembered for That Goal. In some ways it was disappointing he should subsequently notch again, three years later up at Bolton, although nothing will ever detract from the sheer communal joy triggered at Vicarage Road on Monday, December 7 2009, when Radek Cerny became the first Football League keeper ever to retrieve a Doyley effort from the back of his net. The presence of the Sky cameras, most unusually, added to what felt almost universal delight at his achievement, in particular allowing us to marvel at the entirely fitting and predictably uncoordinated goal celebration which followed his flying header. I'd forgotten that Jim Magilton was in charge of the hapless QPR side which provided such helpfully lame opposition that night. I wanted to believe Lloyd had notched against a Neil Warnock side. Sadly though 'Colin' didn't appear on the Rangers scene for another few months, denying me the opportunity to suggest that five years later he snapped up our man as a prolific goalscoring defender. However subsequent events suggest our favourite pantomime manager may just have been watching.

We somehow managed to maintain a series of creditable mid-table finishes, most notably under Dyche in 2011-12 when, despite the embarrassing Bassini sideshow, Doyley made his customary 33 starts as we garnered 64 points and a praiseworthy 11th place finish. At which point the safe remained locked, the Pozzo family rode into town and everything changed, quite possibly for ever.

Despite Gianfranco Zola and Lloyd Doyley occupying, from

a playing perspective, non-overlapping planetary systems, they struck up a sound working relationship with Lloyd remaining a regular during the run to ultimate Wembley disappointment at the hands of Palace. The first Palace disappointment, that is.

We were, by then, approaching the beginning of the end for Doyley. At first Beppe Sannino usually picked Lloyd but the disjointed 2014-15 combination of Sannino, Garcia, McKinlay and Jokanovic had little time for our man, granting him just five starts as promotion was finally secured, with Lloyd suffering progressively from a series of nagging injuries.

He made his final Watford start on Boxing Day 2014, in a 1-0 home defeat at the hands of Wolves and the last of his nine international appearances for Jamaica during the same month. His last bench appearance for the club followed a few months later, at Derby.

After a series of false alarms – Charlton, QPR, Gillingham, Bristol City and probably others – Lloyd finally took his boots to Rotherham of all places and Warnock of all managers. He signed a short-term deal in mid-February, with the Millers staring down the barrel, looking destined for the drop. Having arrived on a Friday, desperately short of match practice after well over a year without a first-team start, Lloyd went straight into Warnock's team the following day, making a home debut against Burnley.

Things could have gone better. Lloyd conceded a penalty as his new club lost 2-0 to Dychey's erstwhile champions. However by the end of the season the Millers had put together a remarkable ten-game unbeaten run, moving ten points clear of the relegation zone, leaving Warnock to be hailed as some kind of Red Adair-style managerial genius. Lloyd's contribution to their great escape was, in reality, limited.

In an ideal world he would have appeared every week and helped transform a wobbly rearguard into an impregnable defensive blanket. Sadly though he only actually played twice more, although both were victories, with his final Millers appearance coming in a pulsating 2-1 win over local rivals Leeds United.

Seemingly it won't be at Rotherham, but wherever Lloyd turns up in 2016-17 you can rest assured he'll do a decent job. Just like he always did.

How many times can you recall seeing a flying opposition winger, earmarked as a potential dangerman, quietly ushered by Doyley into an unthreatening cul-de-sac out towards the corner flag? It was simply what he did.

But to say Doyley was universally popular around The Vic, certainly in the early days, would be a million miles from the truth. In fact there were times when he made that 'butt of the crowd' position his exclusive property, but then we've always been hardest on our own. Callaghan, Jonno, Gifton and dozens of others over the years have all received far more than the stick they'd have collected if we'd signed them on the open market.

You possibly spotted Lloyd at Quique's last match. He was wandering around in front of the Elton John Stand, wearing a New York Yankees pin-stripe top, emblazoned with 'Jeter' on the back.

I'd love to think the finest shortstop ever to play baseball is, in his retirement, strolling around Florida wearing a Watford shirt with Lloyd's name proudly displayed.

Doyley did divide opinion but we all watched the same performances out there. There's no mystery regarding his contribution to the cause. It's simply that Watford fans saw and valued that contribution very differently.

Some saw an ungainly liability who fell over a lot and couldn't pass the ball in a straight line to save his life. They saw a player who was all knees and elbows and that made him the easiest scapegoat imaginable. These people tended to shout at Lloyd, wave their arms around and get angry because they focused on his flaws rather than his qualities.

Others saw simply the best man-to-man marker at the club, who also happened to epitomise so many good things about Watford Football Club as it endured what could justifiably be called A Difficult Time, in that we were hopelessly skint and usually lost.

I sit firmly in the latter camp but for me Lloyd represented a precious link between Old and New Watford. He was a far better player than he sometimes looked, while his mistakes invariably appeared much worse than they actually were. There's nobody like that left at the club any more.

There was something of the Ian Botham about Lloyd. Whenever he was out there, things happened. He may not have been directly involved, but they were going on all around him. He was an unwitting catalyst.

From that slapstick Issa stretcher incident on his debut, through his own priceless wrongful dismissal against Leicester in 2012, to the most astonishing piece of wizardry in his very last game when Lloyd, bizarrely hanging about in the opposition penalty area, set up Ighalo to hit the crossbar having played the striker in with the most outrageous flick between his own legs... Stuff just happened when Lloyd was around.

Life without Lloyd will go on just fine. It already has. But it won't be the same. It will be more professional, more serious, more proficient, more skilled, more polished... and not quite as much fun. I'll miss him.

David Harrison is approaching 60 years of supporting the club, from Holton to Deeney and hopefully beyond. After 40 years' strolling through Oxhey Park to The Vic, he recently relocated to West Devon, making the matchday journey more challenging. David worked for various broadcasters and has contributed to *When Saturday Comes* for many years, predominantly covering Watford.

11

For most of his time at Watford, **Lloyd Doyley** wore the number 12 shirt. That was somehow fitting, because he was one of us – the 12th man – our representative on the pitch.

Only four other men have pulled on a Watford shirt more often than Doyley.

But when the end came, he didn't get a chance to tell the supporters what his 14 years at Vicarage Road meant.

So this is it, his letter to the fans…

A LETTER FROM LLOYD

BY LLOYD DOYLEY

I didn't get a chance to say goodbye – not properly, anyway. I was on the pitch when we celebrated promotion to the Premier League in May 2015 and although I hadn't played since Boxing Day I felt as much a part of it as anyone because this is my club. I'd watched the games during the run-in and felt the same nerves as all of you. During the week before that Sheffield Wednesday match, Troy Deeney had come to me and said, 'Lloyd, when we win the Championship trophy, I want you to lift it with me.'

That would have been quite something. It didn't quite work out that way but it was still a special day. Troy and Fernando Forestieri poured Champagne over me. As I walked round the pitch, I waved and applauded and, in my head, I was saying goodbye.

I'm sure if you'd taken a moment to think about it, you would have realised it would be the last time I'd be on the Vicarage Road pitch as a Watford player.

But what you might not have known at the time is that I'd suffered a pretty bad neck injury that needed surgery. Once we'd confirmed promotion away at Brighton, I bumped into a few Watford fans who wanted me to play a few minutes against Wednesday on the final day, but there was no way I could have done even if the manager had wanted to pick me.

It was a nice way to sign off, though, knowing the club was returning to the Premier League. That day wasn't about me, it was about my team-mates and all of you, the supporters. I was just happy to be a part of it.

Now is my chance to say goodbye properly.

Thank you for the 14 years I was at Watford as a professional. You saw me come into the team when I was only 18 and you supported me even though I found it quite hard to step up at the beginning. You stuck behind me the whole way – although I'm sure there were a few moments when you were tearing your hair out – but I like to think you recognised that I worked hard every time I pulled on the shirt. I know I gave my best every time I represented you on the pitch because I knew that, if you were in my position, you'd do everything you could to help the team.

During that time, I played 443 first team games – only Luther Blissett, Nigel Gibbs, Gary Porter and Duncan Welbourne have played more – and that is something I am very, very proud of. It's becoming rare for a player to stay at a club for as long as I stayed at Watford. I had a testimonial season, I had 13 different managers, if you count Graham Taylor, who gave me my first professional contract, and Oscar García, who didn't actually pick me during his very brief stay, I had two promotions to the Premier League… and two goals. And, as a defender, I pride myself on the fact I was never sent off for the first team – well, I was, very late in a game against Leicester City but it wasn't actually me who committed the foul, it was Adrian Mariappa, and the red card was wiped out on appeal, so I think I've got a spotless record.

* * *

I gave everything I had to Watford Football Club, and yet Watford Football Club has given me more. I first stepped through the door as an 11-year-old kid who wanted to play football and wanted to be on Match of the Day. I can remember being a youngster, standing in the tunnel at Vicarage Road and waiting for the first-team players to come off the pitch so I could get their autographs. The people I looked up to were often defenders, like Steve Palmer and Nigel Gibbs, and I'd watch them and see what I could learn.

During the most recent summer, I took my 11-year-old son to the Watford open day and saw the look on his face as he met his heroes and handed over his autograph book to get it signed. I can remember that feeling like it was yesterday and I feel very fortunate that I managed to achieve my dream of playing in the Premier League.

I come from a place in Hackney where we didn't have the most money or the best lifestyle but I had two very supportive parents who would have backed me no matter what I had chosen to do. I can remember leaving the house at 6am on a Saturday or Sunday morning when I was 13 years old to get a series of buses and trains to take me to Watford. They knew how hard I'd worked, and the sacrifices I made (such as staying in when my mates went out).

When I was a second year scholar, Graham Taylor put me in the squad for a game against Birmingham City. He was considering using me to mark their winger Stan Laziridis. He didn't pick me in the end but he made it clear I was in his thoughts. A bit later on, Graham asked me to a meeting with my parents and he offered me a three-and-a-half year contract. He could talk for England, but my parents were convinced after a couple of sentences. I remember him saying that signing a pro contract was just the beginning.

At the end of the season Graham Taylor left and Gianluca Vialli came in. There was a lot of change and he brought in nine or ten players from the Premier League and the Italian league. Graham had always given young players a chance but suddenly it seemed like I might have to wait.

The first-team squad went on a pre-season training camp to Italy and they had a few injuries. I'd played well in a few reserve games and so they flew me out before the last friendly with Sampdoria. I trained with the first-team squad and Vialli and his coach Ray Wilkins got to know me.

* * *

Every player remembers their debut because it's one of those unforgettable moments. If you were there, you'll probably remember my debut too. I was the only defender on the substitutes' bench for a home game against Birmingham. Pierre Issa went down and then, as he was being carried off on a stretcher, someone slipped and dropped him. While all this was going on, I had to strip off and get on the pitch and get into position with no time to warm up.

I had to learn quickly, but I had some great people to learn from. Ray Wilkins was a great coach and I felt he helped me a lot. Like a lot of Italians, Vialli wanted to play three at the back, which was new to me at the time. I got to play with Filippo Galli, who was twice my age but had played for AC Milan in Serie A and Champions League finals. His English wasn't great but it was good enough to help me. He was so wise and he read the game so well. There was Neil Cox too, who was very loud, and he coached as he played, which really helped the young players.

Things didn't work out for Vialli and he was replaced by Ray Lewington. Over the next few years, the squad got smaller, the club's finances were squeezed and there was even a time when we had to take a wage reduction to avoid going into administration. I didn't play as many games the second year Ray was the manager, which was disappointing because although I was still young, I felt I had improved.

I did what I've always done throughout my career – I worked hard and I forced my way back in. If you train hard, if you are professional, eventually the manager won't be able to ignore you. Someone will get injured, or lose form, and you'll get a chance. If you let your performances in training drop when you're not in the team, you'll not be ready to come back in.

When Ray left, Aidy Boothroyd came in. We knew a few days before it was made public who the new manager would be, but no one had heard of him! So we did our research. We were really struggling when he arrived and we just wanted to survive but he told us he thought we were better than our position and over the summer he brought in some really good players. Maybe it hadn't worked out for them at other clubs but they were all hungry and had something to prove to themselves. Aidy gave us such belief in ourselves. We were direct, for sure, but we had goalscorers like Marlon King and Darius Henderson, and leaders like Gavin Mahon and Malky Mackay. The play-off final against Leeds at Cardiff was one of the best days of my career, without a doubt.

Now I was a Premier League player – up against great players that I'd grown up watching on TV. I can remember buying Ryan Giggs football boots when I was a kid, and then I was having to mark him. (I didn't get close, by the way!)

I felt we did well that season. We kept 13 clean sheets, if you count the cup matches, but when Marlon King got injured we lost that player who could score out of nothing. Or we lost concentration in the last ten minutes. We were fit, strong and disciplined but the top sides test you every minute of every game with their movement and their touch. They are trying to outwit you all the time and, mentally, that takes its toll in the end. You can play so well for 80, 85 minutes and then a moment's lack of concentration can cost you. Knowing what a top player like Giggs, or Wayne Rooney or Didier Drogba is going to do is one thing, stopping it is completely different.

Mistakes are part of the game – every player makes mistakes in every game, it's how you respond that makes a player. You can't ever let your head go down. I've scored own goals, I've made mistakes that have led to a goal but you have to believe in yourself and carry on playing the right way. If I made a mistake, I'd ask for the ball as soon as possible to get back in the game. It's not easy to forget your mistakes but you have to, otherwise you'll make another one.

* * *

After having a taste of the Premier League, everyone wanted to get back there as soon as possible and we started the season back in the Championship in flying form. We were miles clear but we fell away and no one could put their finger on what went wrong. Aidy got rid of Gavin Mahon, who was the captain, and I think he would admit that was a mistake. It was a hard time because the mood of the club changed. You wouldn't believe the difference in the atmosphere when you win a few games in a row compared to when you lose a couple. You can feel the pressure from the manager because his job is under threat, and you can feel the crowd getting edgy.

In the end, Aidy went and that was when Brendan Rodgers came in. He had a reputation as an excellent coach who'd worked at Chelsea and learned from Jose Mourinho but he'd not been a manager.

When Brendan first came in, he said to me: 'Lloyd, I respect you, but you're not my kind of player. I'll allow you to keep training with the first team but I won't be giving you a new contract.'

That was hard to take because you're not just being rejected but your livelihood is under threat. I didn't like what Brendan said but I didn't have a problem with him because he was honest with me. He didn't tell me one thing and do another.

That was one of the hardest periods of my career because when you know the manager doesn't really want you, it's tough to stay positive. But I say this to young players now, there's no point sulking. Getting angry doesn't help anyone. You just have to train hard and try to work on the things the manager wants you to do. More than ever, football is a squad game – there are more players than there are places in the team, so you have to be patient sometimes.

Brendan realised he had to adapt his football for the Championship. We'd been a very direct team with Aidy and we didn't have the players to do what Brendan wanted. The Championship is about hustle and bustle and fighting for control of the game. You get closed down very quickly all over the pitch, it's nothing like Premier League academy football. I think Brendan knew he had to mix it up a bit.

Eventually I got a chance to play at left-back and, although that was not my preferred position, I gave it my all.

That's where my nickname, Lloydinho, came from. We were playing Chelsea in the fifth round of the FA Cup at Vicarage Road. It was 0-0 and I played a pass with the outside of my right foot, all the way down the channel for Tamas Priskin, and he scored to put us ahead. Although we lost 3-1, I played well, got my place in the team and the gaffer called me Lloydinho in the press conference. At the end of the season, just before he went to Reading, Brendan gave me a three-year contract, so I won him over.

Next up was Malky Mackay, and that was tricky because I'd played alongside him in defence. I kept calling him Malky out of habit and managers don't like that. They want to be called gaffer or boss. I kept saying, 'Malky... sorry, gaffer!' I think if

I'd kept on he'd have started fining me!

I knew when I played with them that both Malky and Sean Dyche would go on to be coaches and managers. They were managers on the pitch really, always talking, always organising.

But both of them had a really hard job because the club was struggling financially again. The budget was being cut and the ambition at the club had gone from trying to get back into the Premier League to trying to stay in the Championship.

We had three managers in six months – Aidy, then Brendan, then Malky – and as players we didn't know where we were. I was one of the more experienced players so I tried to lead by example and make sure that no matter what was going on behind the scenes we worked hard in training.

When Laurence Bassini owned the club it was unsettling because there were all sorts of things rumbling away in the background. As players, you sometimes don't know what to believe. There was a long period where there were rumours of Italian owners coming in.

That summer, we came in to do two weeks training just to keep ticking over, then have another couple of weeks off before pre-season started. Sean didn't know what was happening and he said: 'Look, if I'm here in two weeks then this work will help us all out when pre-season starts. If I'm not here, then this work will do you good anyway.'

When we came back, we eventually heard Sean was going and Gianfranco Zola was coming in. Immediately seven or eight players arrived. I didn't know who a lot of them were, so I was looking them up to see how many of them were defenders.

I'd been injured during pre-season and my testimonial game against Tottenham was my first game back. That's a day I will never forget. It was my testimonial year but I couldn't be certain I'd even be staying at the club. Then, just as the transfer window was closing, another load of players came in.

We had about 42 or 43 players at the training ground every day and it was chaos. Normally a first team squad will be about 22. Zola was trying to get to know the players who were already at the club, and then there were all the new ones coming in, all talking in different languages, some of them barely able to speak English at the time.

It was impossible for Zola to train this huge group so he split it in two and he worked double-time to coach everyone. He'd come in early to take a session with the players who weren't in his first-team squad, then he'd take the normal training session. It must have been exhausting for him but he wanted to treat all his players with respect, even if it was quite obvious that a few would have to go.

I did wonder whether I'd be a Zola-type player but he wanted to play 3-5-2 and I was quite comfortable with that so I was pretty regular in the team. I loved playing for Zola – of all my managers he and Aidy were the best, Zola for the football, Aidy for his man-management and motivation.

Zola wanted us to pass the ball and even though pretty passes weren't really my game, I adapted again and really enjoyed it. That was by far the best team I played in – some of the football was awesome, it felt like playing for Brazil. Almen Abdi and Matej Vydra were among the best to play with because they had the ability but they adapted it to the Championship. People might think that the other foreign players who didn't 'make it' weren't good enough but they were all top quality. But there's much more to settling into a team than just the football. Some of the lads had so much ability but they'd come off after a match and say, 'It's so fast here.' They also had to adapt to the language, the lifestyle and the food as well as the game. Then we had Nathaniel Chalobah protecting the back three. He was only a teenager but he played like an experienced international. He demanded the ball from older players and, as a youngster, that is not an easy thing to do.

The only disappointment was that we didn't manage to get the job done against Crystal Palace. I really felt we were good enough to go up that year and I can't explain what went wrong that day – if I could answer that question, we'd never lose a game again!

* * *

The following season, I thought the players who came in were even better but the team didn't settle. Maybe Gianfranco was too nice. If we are really honest with ourselves, maybe the players took advantage of him a bit much because we knew he wouldn't give us a rocket. Only afterwards did we realise that, but I think we took liberties with him. Maybe we'd turn up a few minutes late when before we'd have been on time. It's little things like that which you don't necessarily realise at the time.

When Beppe Sannino came in it was a real culture shock. He brought all his own staff and everything changed but at the start he couldn't speak a word of English. It was so difficult for us to know what he wanted but he was so passionate. He wanted to express what he wanted but he didn't have the words. Tactically he had very precise ideas – he wanted you two yards this way, or two yards that way, but he couldn't explain it, he'd have to physically put you in position on the training pitch. We couldn't really understand him and the first six months were really frustrating for him.

Then came a crazy six weeks. Sannino went, Oscar Garcia came in but got ill after one match. He was the only manager I had at Watford who didn't pick me! Billy McKinlay had come in as a British coach and when it was clear Garcia wasn't going to come back they made him the manager, but he lasted only two games. I think that was a spur of the moment thing and they didn't think about it long enough but he was a good guy. There was talk Nigel Gibbs was going to come in as a coach but that didn't happen either, and then they appointed Slavisa Jokanovic.

I thought we had a good enough team to go up no matter who the manager was. I played in Jokanovic's first game – a 3-0 win at Sheffield Wednesday – but he dropped me. Then, on Boxing Day against Wolves, he made five or six changes and I came in at left-back. We lost 1-0, I didn't play well, the whole team didn't play well, but I was the one who got dropped. I was in the squad, or on the bench, but I wasn't playing.

That was hard. I was glad my mates were getting promoted but I wanted to be part of it. I knew the end was coming – the players that were getting brought in were better and better and although I was working as hard as I could I knew my time was up, especially if we got promoted to the Premier League.

Then I had my neck injury, which was really strange. No one could tell me when I'd done it. I had a slipped disc in my neck. I had tingles in my arms and hands so I saw a doctor, had a scan, and within a couple of days I saw a surgeon who told me I couldn't do anything except walk. No running, no lifting, nothing, because I could easily make it worse and lose all feeling or power in my arms permanently. I had surgery six weeks later but it's pretty scary having your neck operated on. I knew I would be out for six months but, even though my contract had expired, Watford let me carry on training with them so I could get fit enough to have trials at other clubs.

I watched as more new players came in and the quality was another level again – I thought Étienne Capoue looked excellent. I saw a lot of the games in the first half of the season and I thought Watford would finish in the top ten but I felt other teams figured them out a bit after Christmas.

I had trials at a few clubs and ended up going to Rotherham

but at the end of the season I was back at Watford training to keep fit while I looked for a club.

* * *

I hope my time as a player is not done. By the time you read this, hopefully I will be at another club because although I want to go into coaching eventually, I want to keep playing. Once your playing career is gone, it's gone. I want to keep running out in front of that crowd, whether it's 20,000 people, or 10,000 or 3,000. That feeling is awesome.

My dream would be to come back to Vicarage Road as a player one last time. It nearly happened – I had a trial with Gillingham last season and then they were drawn against Watford in the EFL Cup. Maybe in one of the cups, the draw could be kind for me!

For the rest of my life I will have some great memories of the managers and players. If I had to pick my dream back four, I'd play right-back, of course, with Paul Robinson, Adrian Mariappa and Malky Mackay. It's not an easy choice but the three best forwards I played with were Fernando Forestieri (his ability was ridiculous when his head was right but he picks and chooses his days), Troy Deeney, who is an example for anyone who needs to make positive changes in their life, and Marlon King for his will to win. My three favourite matches were my debut against Birmingham, the play-off final against Leeds, when we just knew we were going to win, and the game against QPR when I scored.

You probably thought I'd forgotten to mention the goal! How could I forget, although I sort of spoiled it by scoring again at Bolton a few years later! The one against QPR was great because it was on TV. A few games before that I'd had a few shots. I was getting forward and cutting inside, but that night we scored a perfect team goal. I passed it out from the halfway line, went up the wing, played a one-two and kept on running into the box. I couldn't believe it had gone in and I thought it might be offside so I looked over at the linesman. I remember Tom Cleverly telling me to go to the Watford supporters to celebrate. They made a T-shirt – and yes, I've got a couple of them at home but it's the memory I'll treasure most.

And last, but by no means least, I'll never forget the fans. I'm one of you now but I'll always appreciate the support you gave me.

All the best,
Lloyd

12

Clarke Carlisle has battled alcoholism and depression for many years and survived an attempt to take his own life in December 2014.

His time at Watford was successful. He was part of Aidy Boothroyd's promotion-winning team, although a clause in his transfer from Leeds prevented him appearing in the play-off final, and made his Premier League debut in Hornets colours.

On a visit to Vicarage Road with Adam Leventhal, Clarke reflects on the progress he has made since attempting to take his own life.

RECLAIMING WATFORD

BY CLARKE CARLISLE WITH ADAM LEVENTHAL

Clarke Carlisle returned to Watford on June 15, 2016.

It was the first time he had been back since he'd survived an attempt to take his own life on December 22, 2014.

This is an account of his emotions and memories as he rediscovered a club and location that had played a key role in his life on and off the pitch.

* * *

Carlisle walks in to an empty Vicarage Road and sits in the front row of the Rookery End to the right hand side of the goal and remembers instantly the feeling of playing on the pitch that is now in front of him.

'When we first walked out into the stand I noticed that it is very different. But I got a really good feeling. I actually miss playing here. I used to really enjoy playing at the Vic. I've got really fond memories.

'Now this will probably be totally inconsequential to anyone who has ever supported Watford, but after being injured for the majority of the 2006-07 season I came in and made my Premier League debut against Portsmouth and about 50 minutes in I put in the best tackle of my career, on Lomana Lua Lua on the halfway line.

'The ball was coming into him and I was running towards him from behind and he didn't look over his shoulder and I vividly remember thinking, "He doesn't know I'm coming. If he doesn't look in the next half a second he's having it." To my delight he didn't look, tried to open out to take the ball in his stride and I just came in at full pelt and absolutely lifted him.

'I took the ball out, took him out, he got a bit of "Air Jordan hang time" and it got a mighty roar from the crowd. That was the single most satisfying tackle in my career. I'd been out for so long, I thought the Premier League was going to pass me by.'

Prior to that first Premier League appearance and tackle, he'd been out injured for eight months. Before he played for Watford again, Aidy Boothroyd, the manager, sent him out on loan to Luton Town.

'Aidy said, "Go out on loan, get some games." The fact that it was at Luton was perfect; I was living in St Albans. The only thing in my head was that the Luton fans might give me some stick when I was there – which I didn't care about. I hadn't sold my soul; I did it in order to do better for Watford.

'I had had a really complex injury. It was in my hip flexor and we treated it as a grade two torn flexor. The scan showed a normal torn muscle. We'd rehab it and get back into training but as soon as I'd got to full training it would break up again. This happened three times; the physios didn't understand what was going on.

'I went to see a specialist who said, "Have you had it x-rayed?" "I said, of course not, it's a muscle injury." But instead of repairing with muscle there was bone growing in there. It looked like torn muscle on the scan but it was actually bits of bone in a little hole. I could rehab it to a certain extent but as soon as I asked for full exertion it would break down. It was so frustrating, one of the most frustrating injuries of my entire career; I had to go on pills to decalcify my body for two months, and I couldn't do any exercise whatsoever because all my bones were brittle. I was depleting my calcium supplies.

'I then had to have another x-ray to check that the little bits of bone were gone. Then I had to recalcify my body and then get back into training. That was a bit worrying. I had to check if my bones were ready or not. I tested everything in that tackle – especially my psychological willingness to go into a clash of bodies. I was a happy man.'

He soon remembers the testing moments that he endured on the road back to fitness watching the team. He looks to his right and pictures the old East Stand, where Aidy Boothroyd would often require non-playing squad members to sit and watch the action.

'Frustrating doesn't even begin to cover it. There were times where I didn't want to be here. If the lads aren't doing well, you just want to be out there to contribute, not thinking you'd be the difference but you want to be contributing and fighting for the cause.

'My livelihood was on the line but it was totally out of my hands. I'm sat in the stands watching these eleven guys give their all. When Kingy hits the post, when Youngy sticks one over the bar, when we batter teams for 20, 25 minutes and don't score and then concede one on the break, I was seeing my livelihood drip away. Not only my personal career and status of being a Premier League player, but the potential for me to step on and earn for my family, and step up to that next level in the footballing hierarchy.

'I definitely did have dark moments, but I didn't know that it was a dark moment to be acknowledged and dealt with. Looking back I can see times where I was really not wanting to go into training, making sure I was in treatment for the shortest possible time so I could either go home or go out for a long period.

'I can remember going out in Watford on my own for a few nights in a row, spending a lot of time on my own, isolating myself. I wasn't going out on a bender but just going out on my own, having half a dozen pints and getting away from anyone and everyone.'

He had feared being isolated when he moved away from his family in the north of England to move to Watford. The reason he had made the switch was due to his relationship with Boothroyd, with whom he'd built a strong bond while the pair had been at Leeds. The then first team coach was given his big opportunity to manage for the first time at Vicarage Road.

'I was buzzing for him. He was finally acknowledged for the qualities he possessed rather than being undermined on a daily basis. I didn't have a great relationship with Kevin Blackwell and my personal opinion of him was that he was disrespectful to his coaching and playing staff. Aidy bore the brunt of that, so we had a common focus: if ever we were in charge we'd do it a different way. I remember texting him, "How the bloody hell have you got out!"'

Carlisle's face lights up as he sings 'Please release me, let me go!' recalling the feeling he had when Boothroyd left to go to Watford. He would follow him, but not before he'd scored a decisive goal for Leeds at Vicarage Road in April 2005.

'No matter how friendly you are with someone, I'm playing against him so I scored a goal against him for me and for my team. Aidy said I celebrated like I'd won the FA Cup! But it was a last-minute winner and I'm a centre-half and we don't score many!

'Throughout the season, before I'd talked to him about everything – the missus, the family, the personal situation – and he was hot on psychology so he was really interested in the stuff I was learning about addiction.

'We had lots of deep and meaningful conversations. He knew where I was at, knew I wanted to be up north and it was a big thing to ask me to come to Watford. He showed how willing he was. He was incredible.

'Summer of 2005 he had heard that I was going to Stoke so I don't know whether that kicked him into action or if he was going to do it anyway. I was on the way to Stoke and he said, "Whatever you do, don't sign anything and come and speak to us."

'In the conversations we had had over that year, he'd got to know me as a person. He knew my reasons for going here or there, the qualities within me to combat what I was going through. He had the measure of me as an individual before he signed me. The only reason I came to speak to Watford was because it was Aidy. If there had been any other manager in situ here I would not have been speaking to them.

'I remember my first goal against Derby only because I gave Aidy a hug after it and he gave us three days off. I ran straight over, gave him a hug and the boys battered me. I never did that again, but it was one of those moments. "You did the right thing bringing me here and I repaid the faith you showed in me by contributing at this end of the pitch as well. That one's for us!"'

Carlisle then heads into the dressing room at Vicarage Road. The contrast to the home facilities when he had been at the club couldn't be starker. An expanse of perfectly lit black and chrome greet him. Space, luxury and care; the trademarks of the new changing rooms.

'It's incredible! This is a totally different stratosphere. The changes we made first time around getting into the Premier League were exciting but this is taking a club to a new level, not simply fixing something to make it nice or painting over cracks. This is Premier League, next generation.

'The majority of my career wasn't spent in dressing rooms like this: Loftus Road, Bloomfield Road, old Vicarage Road, Sixfields. The only time I got into rooms like this was away in

the Premier League, the Millennium Stadium and Wembley. I
was never blessed enough to have this, but it feels like coming
to Wembley being sat in here.'

The mention of the Millennium Stadium triggers thoughts
of the 2006 Play Off Final in which Watford beat Leeds 3-0 to
win promotion to the Premier League. Carlisle was forced to
play the role of dressing room motivator that day. The reason:
a contractual clause that meant he couldn't face his former side.

'It was ridiculous. I'd never heard of it on a permanent
transfer before, only on loans where you can't play against your
parent team. I don't know who suggested, Ken Bates or Kevin
Blackwell, but it was a sticking point in the deal. They would
not let me go unless I agreed to it and it added to the ire and
the bitter memories that I had at Leeds. Who does it? It's a
restriction of trade; it's bitter and twisted. If they don't want me
any more then let me go. They shouldn't throw spanners in to
hold me back from an occasion.

'I was envious then and fiercely envious to this day of Jay
DeMerit who scored. What if I had scored, in a play-off final?
The fact the lads were successful is what makes it just bearable.
Had they lost I would have been gutted on so many levels.'

After a short time in the dressing room that had got
Carlisle's mind whirring, it's time for lunch after a walk from
Vicarage Road into the town centre.

He sits in a traditional Italian pizza restaurant facing out
towards the pedestrianised high street remembering what life
was like and what he was like when he'd been in Watford some
ten years before.

'I wasn't happy. I see that in a lot of my Watford pictures of
that season, 05-06 when we went up. Professionally I was really
enjoying it but it wasn't a happy time for me personally.

'I'd started drinking again after being sober for a couple of
years after being at the clinic. I'd started drinking at Leeds and

brought it down with me. Money was tight; we were renting in Abbots Langley. I was trying to pay off debts that I already had. It wasn't a good time, that year.

'Looking back I can see that I was living with depression then and didn't know it. I was escaping from that emotional turmoil in whatever way I could.

'Even during that period when I wasn't drinking, I was still going through these depressive episodes and I had no escape mechanism, it would make the depression worse. There was still some kind of explosive reaction or complete isolation like locking myself away in the house for days, something to get away from that state of depression and torment.

'When I first found out about alcohol at 13 or 14, the first thing I did was have a whole bottle of vodka to myself. Every time I went out I had as much as possible because I knew I couldn't drink for three weeks because my parents were so restrictive about when I could go out. In academia it was the same; I would read encyclopedias front to back, as much as I could.'

That was then for Carlisle, this is now. This is living after an attempt to end his life.

'I date everything from 2014 now. I enjoy talking about what is as opposed to what was.

'When I was in a depressive episode and drinking to escape, that was the problem. I'm fed up of playing that game, I know I am more comfortable and in control and better without it, rather than having to question why I am drinking all the time. I don't enjoy it at all.

'The awareness is key. It's like diabetes, where every day you are conscious of your intake. Every day I'm conscious of the fact I am living with depression that can affect me in certain ways.

'I would rather not use a coping strategy. There are certain

emotions that I have always struggled to deal with and wanted to run away from, and either totally ignored or suppressed.
Now I try to make myself feel them, rather than being scared
of feeling them.

'I know there are uncomfortable emotions that I need to
experience. I acknowledge it: "That has made me feel really
sad." If I want to cry that's okay. If I need someone to help me,
that's okay as well. I have an emotional awareness I never had
before but it doesn't always happen like that.

'Sometimes loads of things go on at once and my head is
really loud. Sometimes I can't put music on, there's too much
in my head. I try to centre myself. If I get an opportunity I'll
sit in the garden, have a cigarette and just listen, just be. Sometimes I can't even do that so I play Candy Crush, or Scrabble,
or Championship Manager. If I get to a point where they're not
enough, I know I need to talk to the psychiatrist, to act and get
some outside help.'

The scars inside and out from December 2014 still frame
his face and his life, but he's a university lecturer now and he's
set up a foundation for dual diagnosis for those suffering with
both mental health issues and addiction. He has a future.

'I'm far more appreciative of life in general. Doing the London Marathon this year was a celebration of the fact I can still
use my legs. Remember, I was hit by a ten-tonne truck at 60
miles per hour and I can still run around and breathe.

'My life is full of possibilities not restrictions. I'm open to
whatever may be as long as I've got a thread running through
it which is what the job at university has given me – a standard
employment contract and a new set of students every year.

'Red-letter days, I'm having many of these. I'm in a new
relationship; we're reclaiming places. This is the first time I've
been back in Watford and the town centre since the question-
able period with the ups and downs. Coming back here with

these eyes, I can reflect on what was and acknowledge what is. 'Wonderful. I've reclaimed Watford today.'

Clarke Carlisle joined Watford in 2005 and played a part in Aidy Boothroyd's promotion campaign. He made his first Premier League appearance in Hornets colours and went on to play for Burnley, again winning promotion to the top flight.

13

Adlène Guedioura's thunderbolt shot at the Emirates Stadium clinched victory over Arsenal in the FA Cup quarter-final on a day that will go down as one of the greatest in the club's history.

Mike Walters tells the story of how a bit-part player created one of the moments of the season and the Hornets reprised the 1980s, when they used to dominate encounters with the Gunners.

ADLÈNE GUEDIOURA: A SHOT IN THE DARK

BY MIKE WALTERS

History has a stealthy knack of repeating itself in football, even when original classics and thrilling sequels are separated by 29 years. To win one FA Cup quarter-final at Arsenal in 1987 was satisfying; to see it happen again in 2016 felt like vindication of following Watford through the rapids and backwaters of all points along the river in between.

At face value, there were similarities between the two moments in time. When Graham Taylor's side stormed the marble halls of Highbury, both teams were in the top flight, Arsenal's pursuit of three trophies was tapering towards more modest ambitions, and it was probably a good time to catch them. The Gunners had come through a trilogy of tense League Cup semi-final meetings with Tottenham, prevailing after a replay at White Hart Lane, and amid the bragging rights there had been signs of battle fatigue.

Almost three decades later, Arsenal rang in 2016 with a potential shortage of ribbons to adorn Premier League, Champions League and FA Cup silverware. Damaging home defeats against Swansea and Barcelona, however, had left them ripe for a third consecutive loss at the Emirates for the first time since their move to Ashburton Grove in 2006. Again, the Hornets picked a propitious day to help Arsenal's season unravel like a toilet roll in the wake of a puppy's household exploration.

Give or take a pleasing result, in truth the similarities end there. During Taylor's first incarnation as a messiah at Vicarage

Road, he took more points off Arsenal than any other club in the top flight. Twelve months before the sides met in the FA Cup quarter-finals, the Hornets had even demolished them on consecutive days in 1986, following a 2-0 win at Highbury on an Easter Monday lunchtime with a 3-0 success at the home of football barely 30 hours later, a fixture rearranged after the original date on Boxing Day was postponed because of snow. Young Welsh striker Malcolm Allen scored in each game, his first goals for the Hornets. It was amusing propaganda to boast that Watford used to beat Arsenal every day of the week. Even when Taylor departed for Aston Villa, and Dave Bassett steered the ship expertly towards the icebergs, the Golden Boys took six points off their favourite stooges in the doomed 1987-88 campaign.

But for Quique Sanchez Flores, the urbane Spaniard negotiating his first season in English football, there were no such portents to offer him an emotional crutch. Since 1988, Sky TV money had widened the gap between aristocrats and peasants, and Watford's results against Arsenal had read like a threatening letter.

Admittedly, either side of the millennium, the Gunners had been fortunate: at Highbury, their goalkeeper Alex Manninger laid out Wembley play-off hero Allan Smart with impunity, his body smash from the same coaching manual as German Toni Schumacher's reckless challenge on French defender Patrick Battiston at the 1982 World Cup; and in the return fixture, Patrick Vieira's dangerous liaison with Heidar Helguson was also as brazen as it was laughably swept under the carpet. To call the incident a clash of heads, as some did, was like describing a boxer's knockout punch as a collision between fist and chin. 'If Vieira had done that to a man in the street, he would have been asked to accompany the local constabulary to the police station to assist them with their enquiries,' fumed Taylor.

As Sanchez Flores prepared for his first FA Cup quarter-final, however, the most recent evidence, in the Premier League at Vicarage Road five months earlier, suggested he was on a hiding to nothing. Watford gave as good as they got for an hour before they folded in Arsenal's blitz of three goals in 12 minutes. At 13-2, odds on the Hornets reaching the semi-finals were tempting for a two-horse race, but they were also a fair reflection of Watford's distant chances – not least because Sanchez Flores had not even known which team he was planning to upset until four days before the tie.

Ludicrously, Arsenal's fifth round replay at Hull was delayed until the Tuesday night before FA Cup quarter-final weekend, ostensibly because of fixture congestion but, in essence, because English football's governing bodies remained in thrall to the annual monument to tedium known as the Champions League. Somewhere in the smallprint, there was a clause about Premier League clubs not being allowed to play at the same time as Champions League fixtures in case the alternative source of entertainment affected TV ratings. The paranoia behind such garbled logic is breathtaking.

BT Sport, who had chosen to screen Watford's quarter-final, were hedging their bets. Not only did Hornets fans not know which club they would be playing – they did not even know which date they should keep clear in the diary. Would it be a 12.30pm kick-off by the Humber on the Saturday lunchtime or a 1.30pm start in north London the following day? As usual, the fans who attend these games, and make the televised spectacle look good by filling the stadium, were last to be considered in the equation. As it transpired, Arsenal won the replay comfortably and the Hornets were allocated 9,000 tickets, spread across two tiers at the Clock end, for their crusade at the Emirates. It was no small achievement that, with only four days' notice, they managed to sell all but 600 of them.

* * *

If ever there was going to be a good time to annoy Arsenal-supporting editorial allies in the *Daily Mirror* office with a nostalgic throwback to 1987, this was it.

Whenever Watford's stars aligned with the Gunners' constellation, your correspondent was never slow to antagonise colleagues with reminders of beating Arsenal every day of the week in 1986, or tales of John Barnes and David Bardsley leading Viv Anderson and Kenny Sansom a merry dance the following year.

Watford's 3-1 win in the FA Cup at Highbury in March 1987 was the stuff of classic bar stool arguments. Where blinkered Gooners swore they were robbed in a late penalty controversy, most of us saw only Niall Quinn backing into Steve Sims and flouncing in the hope referee Brian Stevens would fall for it. Where most of us saw one team playing to the whistle, and another committing one of football's cardinal sins by downing tools, Arsenal cried foul. Where most of us saw resolute defending under siege, Steve Williams saw fit to squeal in Graham Taylor's face like spoiled brat Violet Elizabeth's tantrum in *Just William*: 'I'll scream and scream and scream until I'm sick.'

In a halcyon era when FA Cup quarter-finals kicked off at 3pm on a Saturday, a rare mistake from John McClelland gift-wrapped Ian Allinson the chance to fire Arsenal in front. Goals either side of the interval from Luther Blissett and Barnes, both set up by Bardsley's irresistible service from the right flank, put the visitors ahead and Watford were holding firm, if not riding their luck, when linesman Graham Crafter flagged for a perceived incident in the box as Quinn backed into Sims with time running out.

Stevens did not acknowledge his assistant's semaphore and, as Arsenal stood still expecting a reprieve from the penalty spot, Blissett raced clear to score to clinch Watford's place in the semi-finals.

Blissett, picking up Gary Porter's clearance on the halfway line, hesitated momentarily. 'I had an acre of green grass in front of me and no Arsenal players for company because they had all stopped, waiting for the referee to blow for a penalty,' he said. 'I was only a few yards from the dugouts, and over my left shoulder I could hear this voice – it was the boss, shouting at me to keep going, so I got on my bike and ran half the length of the pitch unaccompanied. I had missed a chance to put us 3-1 up on the break a few minutes earlier, but this time I had enough time to take two bites at the cherry.'

Although John Lukic parried Blissett's first effort, he managed to smuggle the rebound past the retreating Tony Adams on the line. For a few seconds, Blissett's celebrations were suspended as Stevens, confronted by an angry picket in red shirts and white sleeves, went back to consult Crafter, but the goal stood and, in the kindergarten, Williams flung his toys out of the pram, most of them directed at the Watford manager.

In the build-up to the game, Taylor had objected to the appointment of Stevens, who had controversially sent off Hornets goalkeeper Tony Coton in Arsenal's 3-1 win in the League at Highbury six months earlier. Taylor's representations to FA headquarters at Lancaster Gate proved futile, but through his red mist, Williams was convinced the episode had influenced the referee's handling of a Cup tie's dramatic climax.

'One memory that will never go away was of Steve Williams losing it with Graham Taylor and carrying on after the final whistle,' said Blissett. 'Steve was one of the Arsenal players standing on the halfway line, pointing towards the linesman, when I broke away to score, but from an early age you are taught to play to the whistle and Arsenal just stopped.

'I'm not sure what we were supposed to have done wrong because it was never a penalty in the first place. It would have been totally unjust if it had been given. Where was the Watford player committing a foul when the ball came into our box? There wasn't one, it didn't exist. Argue all you like about who had the most pressure or the best chances, but we were resilient and our wingers were magic that afternoon. When I look back now, it also makes me a bit nostalgic – because it was my last memorable cup tie with a happy ending as a player under Graham Taylor, and he managed a few at Watford, didn't he? A couple of months later, he went to Aston Villa and the chapter ended.'

From his pulpit on *Match of the Day* later that night, the high priest of football himself, the late Jimmy Hill, conducted an outstanding forensic autopsy of Arsenal's grievances, concluding that Stevens had made a correct call on the pivotal decision and noting the referee had a much clearer view of the contentious incident involving Sims than his linesman.

If Arsenal were thirsty for reprisal, they only had to wait a week to exact it. No contraption in world football is more mischievous than the fixture computer, and seven days after the stormy finish at Highbury, when coins rained down on Watford's players and coaching staff from the posh seats, the teams met again at Vicarage Road in the League. The Hornets prepared for it by honouring a long-standing commitment to play an exhibition match in the Caribbean before flying home to extend Taylor's record, against gilded opponents, to seven wins and a draw in their last 11 meetings.

Porter recalled: 'On the Monday morning we flew out to Trinidad to play against Sao Paulo of Brazil in a prestige friendly and we lost on penalties, which was no disgrace. The Brazilians were a bit handy – I think Careca was playing for them – and we didn't get home until the Thursday morning after flying through the night. On the Friday morning we had a light training session and on the Saturday, a week after knocking them out of the cup, we beat Arsenal 2-0 in the league. Little old Watford didn't bow down to the big clubs, and the big clubs didn't always like it when we refused to bow and curtsey for them.'

* * *

More in hope than expectation, and many of them clinging to fond memories almost three decades old, 8,400 Hornets were eager risers on Sunday, March 13, 2016. As an early-spring nip in the air gave way to wintry sunshine, it felt like a good day to make a north London tribe blub into their replica shirts.

The build-up, shortened as it was, included Troy Deeney's revelation that his six-year-old son, Myles, was suffering from pangs of divided loyalties on his first visit to the Emirates. 'It doesn't matter if Daddy's playing – he wants Arsenal to win, like they do on FIFA,' said the Watford captain. 'It's all part of being a parent and you've got to live with it. No pocket money this weekend, though!'

Deeney had been frustrated that Sanchez Flores deployed him in a withdrawn role against Bournemouth a fortnight earlier, on the day England coach Roy Hodgson came to Vicarage Road to run the rule over him as a potential latecomer to auditions for the Euro 2016 finals. A turgid 0-0 draw did nothing for Deeney's international ambitions and it was the first of three consecutive games in which the Hornets failed to score ahead of their date at the Emirates, the others being an undeserved 1-0 defeat at Old Trafford and a more laboured performance, with a similar outcome, against shock Premier League leaders Leicester City. The spasms of intuitive, clinical, counter-attacking football which produced four consecutive wins before Christmas, including a memorable 3-0 demolition of Liverpool, had long subsided. Instead of surging beyond the magic 40-point mark, Watford were only grinding towards safety.

In truth, it was becoming a tough watch. Even the fifth-round win against toothless Leeds United in the cup was clinched by a hapless Scott Wootton own goal but, as the great philosopher Arthur Daley once observed in *Minder*, one man's chicken kiev is another man's chicken in a basket. If Sanchez Flores showed little inclination to discard his compact 'block' in favour of a more adventurous approach, pragmatism had its virtues.

So when the teamsheets were published, an hour before kick-off, there were gasps of astonishment on the Emirates concourses when Sanchez Flores made two unexpected calls. In goal, Heurelho Gomes was in the starting line-up ahead of Costel Pantilimon, the 6ft 8in Romanian international who had arrived from Sunderland for a nominal fee two months earlier. Pantilimon had kept clean sheets in the two previous rounds against Nottingham Forest and Leeds, and he had been nominated by the club to do pre-match interviews with the national media during the week. All the signs had pointed to Pantilimon being used as Watford's specialist cup keeper, and although he was devastated when the teams were published, he hid his disappointment like a trooper. 'It was a big game, and I did not want to rock the boat an hour before kick-off,' he said later. 'But I had trained as part of the first team group all week, I thought I was playing.'

Ever the professional, Pantilimon went through the pre-match warm-up routine diligently before the players returned to the dressing room for Sanchez Flores to issue his final instructions. There were barely ten minutes to kick-off, as the Hornets' head coach reasserted the required shape and game plan to defend Watford's 18-yard area, when his fundamental mistake on the teamsheet – subsequently explained as an 'administrative error' – came to light.

Sanchez Flores always used magnetic counters, each one bearing a squad number, on the whiteboard to illustrate his selection and tactics. The teamsheet, usually filled in and signed by his trusted assistant Dean Austin, would be copied from the numbers displayed on the whiteboard. Since No.1 appeared at the apex of the team formation, the name Gomes was duly assigned to the master teamsheet. Sanchez Flores simply did not notice he had left No.1 on the board, instead of supplanting it with Pantilimon's No.18, which was his intention all along. Only when players interrupted his pep talk, to ask why he was telling Pantilimon to command his box, did Sanchez Flores realise his oversight.

Modern convention dictates that players injured in the warm-up can be replaced on the nod. Arsenal, however, were under no obligation to let Watford correct a clerical blunder of their own making. The Hornets were fortunate that neither the Gunners nor referee Andre Marriner had any objection to their careless housekeeping being rectified, and Pantilimon was duly restored to the starting line-up at the last minute.

But there was another name in Sanchez Flores's chosen XI which raised more eyebrows than a Groucho Marx gag. Adlène Guedioura, who had signed for Watford on a permanent basis on deadline day the previous August after two hugely influential spells on loan from Crystal Palace, had played only 59 minutes of Premier League football all season and had grown frustrated at his lack of meaningful game time.

Guedioura had been a colossus on the run-in to promotion under Slavisa Jokanovic in 2015, his performances against Derby and Middlesbrough over the Easter weekend bordering on heroic. Sadly for Watford, his second loan expired after the 2-0 win at Brighton which effectively clinched their ascent through the loft hatch on the penultimate weekend of the season. When they were denied the Championship title by Sheffield Wednesday's stoppage-time equaliser on the last day of term, Guedioura's only involvement was to present long-serving match programme sales co-ordinator Mary Davies with a Football League community award on the pitch at half-time. Two years earlier, Mary's 11-year-old daughter Rebecca had been murdered in her bed as she slept. Missing out on a silver pot to Bournemouth is not even in the same league of distress, is it?

If the Gomes-Pantilimon riddle was an innocent cock-up, Guedioura's selection seemed a genuine left-field pick, a shot in the dark by Sanchez Flores. Watford's head honcho always compiled the 'list' for each game based on evidence set before him during the week on the training pitch. The consensus, among both day trippers from WD postcodes along the Hollo-way Road and those tuning into BT Sport's live coverage from their armchairs, was that Guedioura must have performed like Lionel Messi in training.

Although the Algerian international made 23 appearances for the Hornets over the season, most of them were walk-on parts to help run down the clock. But peripheral influence or otherwise, Guedioura had also been an extraordinarily lucky charm. In the calendar year 2015, he only finished on the losing side once for Watford in 20 games – the drab, last-gasp defeat at home to Ipswich on March 21.

Quique Sanchez Flores, however, evidently had reservations about his retention of the ball and defensive discipline in a rigid shape. There was no disputing Guedioura's dynamism and he had a 'good engine', as the managerial cliché goes, but QSF had invested only limited trust in him… until now.

With a Wembley semi-final beckoning, Sanchez Flores

selected four central midfielders – Guedioura, Ben Watson, Valon Behrami and Étienne Capoue – to throw a defensive blanket over the Gunners' expensive cast of creative talents including Alexis Sanchez, who was the Pozzo family's most valuable discovery when they plucked him from relative obscurity in Chile and sold him from Udinese to Barcelona for £23 million.

This was not a game for mavericks to stray from the game plan outlined by Sanchez Flores with those magnetic counters on the whiteboard. This was a task for conformists. And for 88 minutes, his intuitive selection and tactical literacy worked a treat. If you weren't hiding behind the sofa, or watching the last two minutes of normal time plus the five added on for stoppages through your fingers, the cardiologist will see you now.

* * *

From an attacking viewpoint, Watford's first 45 minutes were not much to write home about. There was one sumptuous pass down the inside left channel, with the outside of his boot, from Étienne Capoue to give Odion Ighalo a gallop, only for the Hornets' top striker to run down a cul-de-sac as the unmarked Troy Deeney waited in vain for a pass. Stop me if you've heard that one before.

The other major talking point, as Watford's exercise in containment reached the interval with few major alarms, was how their captain survived an appalling challenge from Arsenal defender Gabriel Paulista unscathed – and how referee Marriner, who had a good view of the Brazilian's reckless, two-footed lunge, failed to blow for a foul let alone dispense a red card. Those incidents apart, plus a goal correctly disallowed for offside against Olivier Giroud and a couple of wasteful finishes by Egyptian midfielder Mohamed Elneny, Sanchez Flores could be well-satisfied at the break that his patent for asphyxiation was bang on schedule.

But five minutes into the second period, it happened.

Eureka, euphoria, you're not singing any more – not that Arsenal fans had broken into song often, if at all. Guedioura, who had also managed to weather a robust tackle from Gabriel before half-time, made his first significant contribution, turning sharply and whipping a cross to the back post, where Calum Chambers just managed to glance it away from Deeney, who was steaming in to meet it behind him.

There have not been many famous exponents of the long throw at Vicarage Road since Lee Sinnott, who played in the 1984 FA Cup final, or the hapless Albert McClenaghan, who decorated his home debut against Southport in April 1978 by attempting a mid-range throw-in, from in front of the old Shrodells stand, and succeeded only in launching himself on to the pitch but leaving the ball in touch. There was also a suspicion that Aidy Boothroyd signed defender Leigh Bromby in 2008 as much for his windmill throw as his distribution with the ball at his feet. But when Nathan Aké, whose season on loan with the Hornets was a resounding success, stepped up to return Chambers's headed clearance into the box, every Watford fan knows what happened next.

Deeney, who should have been the sandwich filling between markers Per Mertesacker and Chambers at the near post, caught the Gunners napping and nipped in front of them both to meet Aké's long throw – which was a pitching wedge towards the six-yard area more than a long iron towards the penalty spot – with a perfect flick. Ighalo, with his back to goal, was being marked touch-tight by Gabriel and there seemed little room for manoeuvre as the ball bounced across his body from right to left. But the Nigerian, whose 'Iggy Chop' party piece had been one of the Premier League's star turns since he left England defender John Stones on his backside on the opening day of the season, had other tricks in his locker. Eight yards out, he swivelled to hook a first-time effort low beyond Arsenal David Ospina's left hand, a classy finish. The ball was past the startled Gunners keeper, deputising for the injured Petr Cech, before he could blink. Ighalo had scored only two goals in 2016, but here was a reminder that champions believe in themselves, even when nobody else does.

In the BT Sport commentary box, pundit Robbie Savage scolded Arsenal's lack of defensive nous, while Gunners legend Ian Wright criticised the lack of communication between Mertesacker and Chambers which allowed Deeney to steal a march on them. To the delirious hordes behind the goal, however, it looked like a clockwork set piece and masterful execution of a half-chance.

For the superstitious, Watford's change strip seemed to be working its magic again. All but one of the club's six wins on the road in 2015-16 to date had been adorned with the all-black away kit, the 2-1 win at Crystal Palace proving the exception. And for Sanchez Flores, taking the lead at the Emirates was a healthy sign. Only once, the undeserved home defeat by Manchester City in the first game of 2016, had he seen the Hornets fail to win after drawing first blood.

For the next 30 minutes, Watford's performance was, by common consent, as measured, and assured, as any against one of English football's big guns this century. Sanchez Flores had switched from blanket resistance to an orthodox, if narrow, 4-4-2 formation at the break, urging his players to take the fight to Arsenal without compromising his sacred 'block' and maintaining his preferred maximum distance of 35 metres between defensive line and strikers.

Ighalo, who had missed a hatful at Old Trafford 11 days earlier, suddenly looked like a gladiator on the warpath again, seeing his volley deflected wide after Deeney met Allan Nyom's deep cross with a header from beyond the back post. Then Aké, released into generous space down the left flank by a neat interchange with his captain, delivered a low centre across the six-yard box and Ighalo, at full stretch, just failed to make decisive contact at the far post.

'You could see the players starting to believe and you could hear that the fans felt the same way,' said Guedioura. 'We knew Arsenal would enjoy lots of possession, and we knew it was important to stick to the game plan and be clinical. We wanted to do something special and now we believed it was possible.'

Although it suited Watford down to the ground that Arsenal continued to play their pat-a-cake football, high on artistic merit but low on meaningful end product, with an hour on the clock the home side came close to an equaliser. Giroud, darting to the near post with Craig Cathcart in close attendance, diverted Joel Campbell's driven centre goalwards but Pantilimon, who had not been required to make a save of any substance, made an instinctive stop with little more than a twitch of his right arm. The true value of Pantilimon's intervention only became apparent moments later in the defining move of Watford's FA Cup run.

Mesut Özil, crossing the halfway line, was crowded out by no fewer than three black shirts – Aké, Behrami and Watson – and as the German World Cup winner conceded possession with a wanton wave of his arms, as if it was someone else's fault he had run up a blind alley, Watson lifted a diagonal pass to Ighalo. With two touches – a neat trap and a cushioned, volleyed pass down the channel – he picked out Deeney's run towards the corner of the six-yard box, although the Hornets skipper had Mertesacker for company.

Now Ighalo burst forward, occupying the attention of two defenders while the labouring Mertesacker ushered Deeney away from goal, out of the shadows cast by the ramparts of Arsenal's Emirates fortress and into a pocket of bright sunlight. Ighalo's unselfish movement off the ball towards the 18-yard area was critical, because one of his escorts was Gunners left-back Kieran Gibbs, who left a yawning paddock of space down Arsenal's left flank. Guedioura spotted the opening and sprint-ed 30 yards into the gap to support his captain, whose routes to goal had all been cordoned off.

'I don't know if Troy heard me, but I was calling out for the ball,' said Guedioura. 'I did not make that run thinking I was going to score, but there was a space and my instinct was to get forward.'

* * *

It had been a largely unfulfilling return to Watford for Guedioura. Palace had been holding out for a £3 million trans-fer fee, for a player who would turn 30 midway through the season, and relegated Queen's Park Rangers had agreed to meet the asking price, as did promoted Bristol City, only for the Algerian international to reject both Championship clubs. Guedioura had set his heart on a permanent move to Vicarage Road, but Watford had offered only £500,000 and owner Gino Pozzo was not budging on his valuation.

Pozzo held all the aces, knowing Palace were looking to shift Guedioura from their wage bill, and the transfer turned into a classic game of deadline-day brinkmanship. Palace blinked first, and a deal – with a heavy emphasis on increments – duly granted the player's wish. 'It was very stressful because I was waiting for so long,' said Guedioura. 'I never even considered, in my own mind, that I would not come back to Watford. I had to fight for it, but the fight had a good ending.'

With Capoue, Behrami and Watson ferreting and foraging

to such telling effect in the early months of the campaign, however, Guedioura would find himself tethered to the bench for
most of the autumn. And on the night of co-ordinated Paris
terror attacks in November 2015, when 130 unarmed civilians
were slaughtered by deranged pond life, he was understand-
ably distracted when his youngest brother was uncomfortably
close to one of the atrocities. At least one of the terrorists had
a ticket to the France-Germany friendly international and was
refused entry to the Stade de France; while the match was in
progress, two suicide attacks and a bomb caused carnage at
a bar near the stadium. Nabil Guedioura was among specta-
tors who were evacuated on to the pitch, while the German
team stayed in their dressing room overnight before they were
cleared to leave the stadium.

'I was in Tanzania with the Algerian squad for a World Cup
qualifier when I received a text from my mum at 1am,' said the
Watford midfielder. 'I was a bit worried because my brother
had sent me a picture of himself from the Stade de France
and I could not sleep. I was like, "Go home quickly, get out of
there". I was very worried.'

Guedioura would have to wait until the FA Cup third round,
against Newcastle United, to make his first start under Sanchez
Flores. 'I was a bit disappointed about not playing that much
because I wanted to contribute more,' he said. 'It's not easy
being in and out of the team, and I wasn't ready for the way
things happened. I was working hard every day, and it's not as
if I didn't deserve to play or anything, but the team was doing
well. You have to understand, be ready to learn, and when I had
the chance to play, I think I did well – but it was not enough.'

It was against this backdrop of frustration that Guedioura
arrived on the edge of the Arsenal box, his run camouflaged
by the shadows, as Deeney shielded the ball expertly from
Mertesacker before rolling it into his team-mate's path. The

speed gun said Guedioura's shot was travelling at 86.4mph when it left his right boot, rising like a firework under the angle of bar and post. Add another 1.6mph to its velocity and it would have been fast enough for a DeLorean to take you back 30 years in Back To The Future. For ballistic value, it was up there with Matej Vydra's rocket against Brentford the previous season, Richard Johnson's volley at Bristol City in 1998 or Jason Lee's stunning half-volley against Wycombe Wanderers the day after Princess Diana's funeral, when the piano soloist from Westminster Abbey himself, Elton John, was among the crowd.

Arsenal goalkeeper Ospina had barely begun his take-off before the rocket arrowed over his left shoulder. If Guedioura's selection had been a hunch, that goal was a shot in the dark like no other.

Behind the goal, the pandemonium was as memorable as it was unrestrained. Watford were two up at the Emirates, and in his enthusiasm to let it all hang out, your correspondent tore his left calf muscle. It was only the second time, in 45 years of supporting the Hornets, that he had suffered physical injury while celebrating a goal. The other was Smart's clinical finish at Wembley in 1999, although the discomfort of strained rib muscles was soothed by local anaesthetic in the party on Watford High Street afterwards. Several pints of local anaesthetic, if truth be told.

Moments later, amid the joyous rituals after Guedioura's missile, a father joined his son and about 8,000 other Watford fans in the communal bounce, hopping on his one good leg. It was a pitiful sight, as was his geriatric shuffle a mile up the Holloway Road to the car afterwards – but it was worth every single painful step.

Racing from the shadows where he had launched his nuclear warhead beyond Ospina, the choreography of Guedioura's celebration had been more co-ordinated. At first, he had sunk to his knees and milked the travelling fans' acclaim like a dairy maid. Then, as team-mates arrived in the sunlight to share his jubilation, the French-speaking clique joined him in a premeditated line-dance celebration.

Was that a whole season's frustration packed into the venom of his shot? 'Not really,' he smiled. 'The manager gave us a plan and we stuck to it well. He did not make a big speech at half-time, he just spoke about a few minor rectifications. When the ball came to me I didn't think too much about anything except a clean strike. From the edge of the box you normally go for power, and often those shots will go over the bar and into the stand because you try too hard, or you do not focus enough on technique. But I will remember this as one of the best goals I've scored and certainly one of the most important. I scored a goal at Cardiff, in one of my first games for Watford, from a similar distance, but this was a special game and it was a great sensation to score in Arsenal's stadium. Maybe the celebration confused some people, but I had been talking about it with Capoue before the game. We were just copying the moves from a band in Paris, but you never expect to do it at an FA Cup quarter-final.

'You can talk about individual players and their impact on the game, but this was not just about my goal – the team was fantastic, the fans were fantastic and the manager's game plan worked. It was a great day for the whole club.'

Of course, the drama was far from over. Arsenal responded to Guedioura's stupendous hit by making a triple substitution and cranking up the tempo. Watford, with Cathcart immense at the back, appeared to have weathered the storm and fewer than two minutes of normal time remained when Danny Welbeck, one of the Gunners' three replacements, exchanged passes with Özil and threaded a neat finish between last defender Sebastian Prödl and keeper Pantilimon. Uh-oh, there was still time for 88 minutes of exemplary application to be undone.

Suddenly, Watford's energy evaporated. Where they had covered so much ground, now they appeared to be stuck on a treadmill. Where they had contained pedestrian opponents, now they were confronted with bravado. Where they had been able to keep the Gunners at a safe distance, now their goal was under siege. And as the clock ticked round to 90 minutes, the Hornets enjoyed a miraculous escape.

Arsenal sub Alex Iwobi's snapshot from 20 yards hit the foot of Pantilimon's right-hand post, the Watford keeper could only shovel the rebound to Gibbs and, when he shifted the ball to Welbeck, the England striker was odds-on to equalise, only for the visitors' goal to lead a more charmed life than a snake in a basket. As Welbeck turned through 270 degrees to complete the formalities, the ball nudged his standing foot and he shanked his effort wide – gloriously, impossibly, thankfully wide – with the goal at his mercy. If it was a miraculous escape, neutrals agreed it would also have been a travesty if Watford's stoicism had been thwarted at the last gasp.

There was still enough time for Welbeck, surging beyond the tiring Prödl, to lift another chance high and wide before Arsenal's 16-game unbeaten run in the FA Cup was over and frayed nerves at the Clock end gave way to unrefined joy.

Que sera sera, whatever will be will be, we were going to Wembley.

The mutual appreciation between players and fans in the post-match debriefing lasted several minutes.

Wastefully, as was the case 29 years earlier, Watford squandered the achievement of knocking out Arsenal in the last eight by turning in a limp performance in the semi-finals.

In 1987, with first-choice keeper Tony Coton already ruled out by a broken thumb, his deputy Steve Sherwood passed a fitness test on a dislocated finger on the morning of the

semi-final against Tottenham at Villa Park, manager Taylor
kicking a ball against his damaged hand as hard as he could
with no ill-effects. Inexplicably, Taylor picked chief executive
Eddie Plumley's son, Gary, who had been signed as emer-
gency cover on non-contract terms during the week, to play
instead of Sherwood. Former Newport County keeper Plumley, who was manager of an Ebbw Vale wine bar at the time,
was a bag of nerves and Spurs won 4-1. He bought a fridge
with his £250 match fee. And for Sanchez Flores, an insipid 2-1
loss against an unremarkable Crystal Palace side at Wembley
was effectively the last of the sommelier's wine in his reign,
defeat exacerbated by stubborn team selection and too many
players' performances nearer chore than privilege.

When the disappointment of another forlorn retreat from
Wembley has subsided, however, Watford should look back on
their first-ever win at the Emirates with pride. Far from being
the short straw, it turned out to be the finest bale in the
haystack.

Like the Arsenal keeper stranded by Guedioura's piledriver,
most of us never saw it coming. But just as the memory of
Highbury in 1987 retains its nostalgic hue, an Algerian's golden
shot in the dark will never lose its afterglow.

Mike Walters is a long-serving sportswriter on the *Daily Mirror*. His
first game as a Watford fan was a 5-0 win against Reading in the
FA Cup third round in 1971.

14

Ciro Scognamiglio is a sportswriter and Napoli fan who watched as Walter Mazzarri created the finest Neopolitan team since the days of Maradona.

Mazzarri's career had barely suffered a hiccup to that point but his reputation was dented by an ill-fated spell at Milanese giants Internazionale.

His reputation as a fiery disciplinarian and a master motivator preceded him to England, but what's he really like?

MAZZARRI

BY CIRO SCOGNAMIGLIO

He has entered into the hearts of Naples and the Neapolitans, yet Walter Mazzarri has never lived in the very heart of Naples, the charming centre of Campania's principal city. That's been his choice: the new Watford manager doesn't like fuss, or the limelight. He's played as a midfielder in many teams, and managed as many again. But perhaps no experience has been as important as the time the coach from San Vincenzo in Livorno spent, between October 2009 and May 2013, in the dugout of Napoli, a team he took to second place in the championship and to victory in the Coppa Italia – not forgetting that Champions League challenge against Chelsea.

It was a quiet love between Mazzarri and Napoli, but still intense, *intensissimo*. He worked a lot, perhaps too much, in the sense that he wasn't able to profoundly enjoy the city. The Napoli team's daily training takes place outside the city, at Castel Volturno, which in fact is in the province of Caserta. Mazzari chose to live in Pozzuoli, not far from the sports centre where he coached football every day, in a very private and quiet countryside villa with a swimming pool. He enjoyed taking walks along the sea shore, but chose the quietest times to do so. The same with visiting the magnificent excavations at Pompeii – he did so, but tried not to mix with people. And he often went to Castel dell'Ovo and the Borgo Marinari – pearls on the Naples coast – but was very rarely spotted. But that didn't mean he didn't have a strong link to the fans at Napoli's stadium, the San Paolo. There is one little known episode. One day, he was driving home from the Castel Volturno training ground, and in Quarto, a district of Naples, he came across a demonstration about landfill. There were hundreds of people. They were angry about the waste crisis, the roads were full of rubbish and there were large, toxic bonfires. This time, someone did notice Mazzarri, despite his car's tinted windows. The Napoli coach could have kept right on going, but he didn't. He started talking to the angry people, listened to their arguments, and convinced them to remove the blockades that they had created. This too is Walter Mazzarri.

He is not interested in being nice to journalists. He prefers to talk about facts, and about his own work. He had a very precise game plan for Napoli – 3-5-2 – and was unlikely to change it. At the start, few believed in it, and others found it too defensive – but no. (An aside: in Italy 3-5-2 was the plan of a certain Antonio Conte, now dedicated to his adventure with Chelsea after leaving the Italian national team, which he deployed to relaunch Juventus.)

Mazzarri's first match in the Napoli dugout was against Bologna, at the San Paolo. The *Azzurri* managed to win 2-1, coming from behind. This would often happen in the Mazzarri era. One unforgettable success came against Juventus in Turin, when Napoli came from 2-0 down to win 3-2; the cries of their 'friends' in the commentary box have gained cult status on YouTube. Perhaps there are stronger tacticians than him, and there are certainly more fashionable managers, who know how to strike the right notes with the media and so appear more likeable, but few know how to motivate like Walter.

And by the way, on the subject of the alleged defensiveness of 3-5-2, under him, Napoli scored very often. It was in precisely this period that Edinson Cavani, who had transferred from Palermo, became a 20-goal-a-season striker, able to make it to Ibrahimovic's wealthy Paris Saint-Germain. Cavani must thank Mazzarri, who usually brings out the best in the centre forwards available to him. It hasn't only happened at Napoli: some years ago the Livornian succeeded in the task of saving Reggina from relegation to Serie B, even starting with a significant points penalisation (minus 15), with Rolando Bianchi as centre forward scoring a lot.

The only disappointment is that, in the Champions League, Mazzarri's Napoli were on the receiving end of a comeback. They won the first leg of their second round tie against Chelsea 3-1, but were then knocked out following a 4-1 defeat at Stamford Bridge. That year Chelsea, managed by Roberto di Matteo, would go on to win the Champions League. Nobody came as close as Napoli to knocking them out. 'I've worked a sporting miracle,' Mazzarri said after Napoli's experience. He found it difficult to criticise his team in public. He defended them no matter what, even when things had gone off-track. If ever there was something to say, he would say it behind the closed door of the dressing room, far from indiscreet ears (i.e. out of the earshot of journalists).

Perhaps his favourite player was Marek Hamsik. Look at these words on the Slovak: 'With 11 Hamsiks in the team Napoli would have won everything, conceding hardly any goals and scoring a lot. We would have been compared to the Dream Team, to the group of dreams, better than the 1992 USA basketball team in Barcelona. Larry Bird, Magic Johnson, Charles Barkley, Karl Malone, Michael Jordan, Scottie Pippen, those people. A class in a pure state, a golden projection from another planet. Staying on that theme, Marek has the vision of the game of John Stockton, the American playmaker, who was the start and sometimes the finish of the action, the person who knew so well where and to whom to pass the ball he could make assists with his eyes closed, but who also managed to get to the basket with his eyes open. Hamsik always knew what to do. He knows he's already a manager, and in fact that will be his future!' The question now is will Mazzarri find another Hamsik at Watford?

It is also worth pointing out the special relationship Mazzarri usually has with the chairmen of his clubs. Take, for example, the Reggina *numero uno* Lillo Foti. There had been a difficult moment and so Walter said that, before making any firing decisions, Foti should watch the game alongside him. Mazzarri explained every single thing to Foti in front of the video recorder. Action by action, minute by minute. He stopped the tape, rewound it, every action was a continuous replay. How did it end up? Foti said this: 'Mazzarri, thank you. I've seen a different match today. I will never send you away before time.'

Mazzarri is a 360-degree manager. This becomes very clear reading his autobiography *The Best is Yet to Come*, written for the publisher Rizzoli with journalist Alessandro Alciato and with a preface by Massimo Moratti, for many years the president of Internazionale. Here is an episode that actually took place when Mazzarri was the manager of Livorno during the 2003-04 season. 'I would do anything to realise players' potential,' Mazzari explains. 'On one occasion I called the wife of Vigiani, a very loyal player I had brought with me from Pistoiese. After an extraordinary start, halfway through the season his son was born: his wife was in Florence, and to stay close to her (but also because his salary wasn't enough to allow him to have an apartment in Livorno) he commuted between the two cities every day, 100 kilometres there, 100 kilometres back − 1,400 kilometres a week. The baby wasn't sleeping, Luca took on every problem, including overnight, and on the pitch he was no longer performing. I understood. He was no longer lucid. He was doing everything in good faith, but I had to balance the books. I decided to call his wife, and found a very intelligent person. I introduced myself and used the formal '*lei*': 'My apologies if I am interfering, *signora*. You are young, and I am a man who has had a son. You must understand that your husband loves you very much, and that he would therefore do anything for his family, however he is also at the height of his career, at a decisive moment. If you love him too, and I don't doubt that you do, you will let him know that you don't need to have him nearby every hour of the day and night.' I repeat it to the players *ad nauseam*. I look at performance, but the moment their productivity starts to fall, it is a right and a duty on my part to go back up the ladder, look for the cause, and not stop. At that point I go into private, and analyse it 360 degrees.' That's clear, isn't it?

Mazzarri is unlikely to get discouraged. He never gives up. Only once did he falter. It happened when he was looking after *Primavera* – youth training – at Bologna, in a season marked by the tragic death of Niccolò Galli, and the serious accident which left another of his players, Enrico Spanarello, in a wheelchair. 'For the only time in my life I thought about stopping, abandoning the world of football. I no longer cared about anything,' Walter later said. This is why he does care about the difficulties – in fact, they recharge him. And this is why he took a break after his experience at Inter, perhaps the only experience with more shade than light in the career of a manager who has left happy memories wherever he has coached. (As well as at Napoli and Reggina, Acireale, Pistoiese and Sampdoria are other examples that spring to mind.) This is another anecdote from his autobiography. 'I was behind the wheel. Gabriele [Mazzarri's son], noticing some strange movements, got my attention. A woman in the next car was waving her arms and seemed to want to talk to me. "Thank you, mister, thank you from my heart." The tone of her voice was high, it carried across the noise of the road, and yet I hadn't quite heard her. "What did you say?" "Thank you, mister, for everything that you've done for my son." "Please excuse me, but who are you?" "I am Ricky Alvarez's mum."

'He was a key player for me at Inter, but the previous season had been booed and whistled. An anti-hero, who people no longer wanted to see on the pitch. "Signora, don't thank me, thank your son. He is behaving exceptionally, I have just done my job." Here is what Moratti said to me when we first met: "Mazzarri, listen to me, do not change." I never could. I owe it to myself. To the people. To Ricky's mum.'

No, Mazzarri will never change. If anything, he will always try to better himself, as he did after the conclusion of his experience at Inter. He humbly came to live in England to learn English. This is how his character is destined to remain. Listen to what he said in an interview with Japanese paper *World Soccer Digest* on his relationship with other managers: 'I start from the assumption that this is a very competitive profession and there is no space for real friendships: I can call a coach I respect if I need to ask him something, if I need to discuss matters on the pitch, but never anything else. It all stops there. I certainly wouldn't create a deep bond with a manager who wasn't managing and who would therefore like to be in my place. We wouldn't be able to tell each other the truth, so everything would be constructed, and therefore false. That's not me. I hate hypocritical relationships and it's therefore better not to have them. I do however have excellent relationships with some very skilled coaches like Ancelotti and others I've had the chance to engage with on the same wavelength. It's a question of respect. If you respect me, I respect you.'

Naturally, there are his critics. He certainly has some. There are those who consider him a provincial manager, not up to leading great teams. Always quick to complain, ready with self-pity and alibis, and to find some outside explanation when things don't go the right way. One of his critics writes: 'Why does Walter Mazzarri continually and obsessively have to remind us that he did this or that? That his seasons are always extraordinary and that, under him, players always do the best in their career? Mazzarri has an inferiority complex. His personal trophy cabinet is almost empty (except for one Coppa Italia). But it's never his fault. Always fighting against the entire world, he has to remind himself and others that he is great.'

Mazzarri is certainly one of those people who is 'always on the case', meaning not giving an inch, always concentrating on the job in hand. In one way the break after Inter was almost beneficial, allowing him to concentrate on himself a little. 'As a manager it is like being in jail. One of the few escapes I can allow myself is to take the car and go for a drive, sometimes a long one, with the music turned up high,' his biography reads. 'It's the most relaxing trip I'm allowed. If I'm happy, I listen to a beautiful, lively, dynamic song, which recharges me, something like *Dov'è l'amore* by Cher.

'*Dov'è l'amore / dov'è l'amore /* I cannot tell you of my love / here is my story. *Dov'è l'amore / dov'è l'amore / non posso parlarti del mio amore / è nella mia storia.*'

Good to know. If things go as hoped, the Watford fans already know which song to dedicate to Walter Mazzari. A manager. A real man, who essentially has this philosophy: 'If my team is worth 100, and I get 90, I have done badly. If it's worth 90 and I get 100, pretty good. If it's worth 100 and I get 100, I've only done what I'm paid for. If it's worth 50 and I get 100... I am Mazzarri.'

Initially, by his own admission, he lived through matches in an all-encompassing, absolute way. He once said that after a match he weighed himself and he had lost 2.5 kilograms. 'During a match I evaporate, I consume myself. After the final whistle I have a level of CPK (an enzyme which indicates muscular toxins) of 1,100 when the average level is around 200. It's as if I had run from the first to the final minute, including injury time.'

And now? 'My way of living through a match,' he explained in an interview with *La Gazzetto dello Sport* in January 2014, 'is still the same, but maybe, if you were to measure it, you'd find a slightly lower level today. The experience, the confidence you get from life, give you exactly this, that is the ability to experience things in a more balanced way. More calmly, if I can put it like that.'

This is the Mazzarri that Watford fans will find: for the most part longing for redemption after the abrupt end of his relationship with Inter. There is also the fresh memory of Claudio Ranieri's feat in bringing Leicester to victory in the Premier League. Watford certainly aren't asking that of Mazzarri, but nevertheless they very much want to have a fantastic adventure, guided by Walter, the man who has come from the sea and wants to conquer England. 'A lot of clubs were interested in me,' he recently said after receiving an award in Amalfi, not far from 'his' Naples. 'Then this opportunity came up. I chose a club, a project that I believe is in line with my footballing ideas. I've rediscovered the enthusiasm of my beginnings, when I was at Acireale.' And so, nothing remains but to start. Once again. With Watford.

Ciro Scognamiglio is a sportswriter for the famous and respected Italian sports paper *La Gazzetta dello Sport*. He's also a Napoli fan and watches matches as often as his job allows.

15

Watford's first victory of the 2015-16 Premier League season was a 1-0 win over Swansea on September 12, 2015. Watford fans were ecstatic.

Most of them, anyway.

Olly Wicken tells the story.

THE LITTLE GUY

BY OLLY WICKEN

PART ONE

Noah hears Daddy's key in the front door. He drops his yellow Lego footballer to the bedroom floor.

'Daddy! Daddy!' he shouts.

He leaps over the Lego stadium Daddy helped him build. He races downstairs to the hall to find out if Watford have won a game in the Premier League at last.

'Did we win?' he asks.

Noah watches Daddy take off the yellow, black and red scarf that Daddy says he's had for more than 30 years. Noah wishes he was old enough to have had a scarf for 30 years. He's not even old enough for Daddy to have taken him to a match yet.

He bounces up and down on the spot.

'What happened, Daddy? Did we beat Swansea?'

Daddy squats down. He wraps Noah in a tight hug.

When Daddy lets go, Noah can see that Daddy has got his sad news face on.

'Sorry, little guy. We lost.'

Noah stamps his foot. He runs back upstairs to his bedroom. He dives onto his bed.

He buries his face into his pillow and sobs.

* * *

Later, Noah is sitting on his bedroom floor. His Lego stadium is a lot smaller than it was. There's a puddle of brightly coloured bricks by the far wall where they landed.

He hears Daddy come into the room.

'You look as if you're still upset, little guy.'

Noah's eyes fill with tears.

'I want Watford to win.'

Daddy sits on the floor next to Noah.

'We all do,' Daddy says. 'But the thing is, we mustn't expect Watford to win all the time. A young Watford fan like you needs to get used to losing.'

A teardrop rolls down Noah's cheek.

'It's only the big clubs who expect to win all the time,' Daddy says. 'Watford aren't a big club. They're a little club. It's important to remember this as you grow up.'

Noah wipes his eyes. He wonders if football clubs grow up too.

He hopes so. It's no fun being little.

* * *

The next Saturday afternoon, Noah and Daddy are at the Intu centre.

Noah asks Daddy if it will say on Daddy's phone if Watford are beating Newcastle. Daddy says yes, but tells Noah he shouldn't expect Watford to win because they aren't as big a club as Newcastle.

'We're not bloody pygmies, though,' Daddy mutters.

Noah doesn't know what bloody pygmies are, but they don't sound nice.

Noah asks Daddy what makes a football club a big club. Daddy uses the words 'historic', 'catchment area' and 'fanbase'.

Noah tells Daddy these words are too big.

Daddy says: 'Sorry, little guy, but it isn't very easy to explain.' Daddy tries again but uses another big word: 'entitled'.

Noah can tell that Daddy doesn't really like big clubs. He asks: 'Are little clubs nicer than big clubs, Daddy?'

Daddy grins. Daddy says Noah has absolutely nailed it.

* * *

In John Lewis, Daddy looks at his phone. He punches the air and shouts: 'Ighalo!' He holds out a fist. Noah bumps it.

In the Apple Store, Daddy looks at a computer. He shouts: 'Ighalo! Again!' He holds out two fists. Noah bumps both.

Noah jumps up and down. He tells Daddy that if Watford are beating a big club like Newcastle then Watford must be a big club now.

This makes Daddy start talking like he does when Mummy says he's 'going off on one'. He says something about fans of little clubs being 'properly grounded human beings', while fans of big clubs aren't. Noah doesn't bother listening because Mummy says she never bothers listening when Daddy's being like this.

Soon, Daddy looks at his phone. He says a bad word because Newcastle have scored.

Noah doesn't like the feeling in his tummy.

Later, on the bus ride home, Daddy looks very happy. Noah asks if it's because Watford have won. Daddy thinks for a moment. He says he hasn't checked. He pulls out his phone. He gets a sad news face. He sighs.

'Two late goals to Newcastle, little guy. We lost 2-3.'

* * *

That evening, Noah pulls his stadium completely to pieces.

After lights out, he hears Mummy and Daddy arguing in the kitchen.

'It's pure deceit,' Mummy says.

'It's necessary,' Daddy says.

'It's cruel,' Mummy says.

'To be kind,' Daddy says.

Mummy calls Daddy a bad name.

Noah turns over and folds his pillow over his ears.

* * *

In the morning, Noah rebuilds his Lego stadium. Bigger is definitely better. In fact, he can't think of anything in life that isn't better when it's bigger. He really hopes Watford grow up. But at the moment it's like they need a magic spell to help them.

Suddenly he has an idea. He goes to his desk and gets a sheet of paper.

He's going to send a letter to the North Pole. He's going to ask Santa to bring Watford a Premier League victory, because it hasn't happened yet and every week it keeps not happening again.

Noah gets out his crayons.

He starts by drawing Santa a nice picture of Troy Deeney.

* * *

The next week, Daddy tells Noah that Watford have lost to Crystal Palace. The week after that, Daddy says Watford have drawn with Bournemouth. Noah thinks this sounds more hopeful.

'Are Bournemouth a big club, Daddy?' he asks.

Daddy laughs.

* * *

Noah's tucked up in bed. He says: 'I can't wait for Christmas, Daddy.'

Daddy doesn't seem to want to talk. He seems annoyed Watford have lost at home to Arsenal – a very big club.

'Yeah, all children say that,' Daddy says, and leaves Noah's room.

But what Noah meant is that he doesn't want to have to wait for Santa to fix it so Watford win.

He picks up his yellow Lego footballer and says: 'How can I make Watford win, little guy?'

The Lego footballer is no help at all.

But by the time Daddy comes back upstairs with a glass of milk for him, Noah has had an idea.

'Take me to a game,' Noah says. 'I'll shout at the Watford players. They'll listen to me and play better. Then they'll win.'

Daddy smiles. He ruffles Noah's hair.

'I can't wait for your first match,' he says. 'You're going to be my best football buddy. We're going to watch Watford together for the rest of our lives.'

Noah's so happy to hear this that he starts jumping up and down on his bed.

'But you need to be a bit bigger before you can go,' Daddy says.

After lights out, Noah's Lego stadium becomes a puddle by the far wall again.

* * *

'Daddy! Daddy! Did we win at Stoke?'

When Noah hears Watford lost 0-1, he growls and runs upstairs.

He grabs a Lego crossbar from his rebuilt stadium and breaks it in two – exactly the way Daddy showed him the real life crossbar would have broken if Matej Vydra's shot at home to Brentford last season had hit the woodwork instead of going in.

Soon he hears Mummy and Daddy arguing again downstairs. They're using more big words.

'It's short-term pain for long-term gain,' Daddy says.

'Long-term disaster, you mean – when the truth comes out,' Mummy says. 'It'll destroy your relationship with your son. Completely. Forever.'

Noah isn't sure what they're talking about. But he wonders if it means he won't be Daddy's best football buddy for life after all.

He puts on his Watford woolly hat and pulls it down over his ears.

* * *

'Daddy, my friend Jacob says Watford beat West Ham 2-0.'

Daddy's eyes widen a little.

'But we didn't, did we, Daddy? We lost 0-1.'

Daddy doesn't look comfortable.

Noah says: 'Jacob's a liar. Lying is definitely bad, isn't it, Daddy?'

Daddy thinks before he answers. He looks Noah in the eye and says carefully: 'It's definitely bad for a child to lie.'

Noah smiles. Daddies are never wrong.

* * *

When Daddy arrives back from the lunchtime home game against Manchester United, Noah rushes up to Daddy to ask the score. Daddy doesn't say the score. He tells Noah the match was on the telly, and he's recorded it so they can watch it as if they were both at the match together. Noah rushes to the sofa so he won't miss a moment.

Manchester United score quite early in the match. Much later, when there's only three minutes left, Troy Deeney scores a penalty to make it 1-1. Daddy says Watford have done very well. Noah shouts and shouts at Watford to get a winner, but Manchester United score in the last minute to win 2-1. Noah bashes the sofa with his fists.

Daddy picks Noah up and sits him on his lap.

'It's good we watched this together, little guy,' he says. 'It tells us something important about life. Even when you don't win, you can still be proud of how well you did. There's much more to life than winning.'

Noah pouts.

He wishes Daddies weren't always right.

His own life has got too much 'much more' and too little winning.

* * *

The next morning, Noah is playing under the kitchen table with his yellow Lego footballer.

Noah hears Daddy enter the kitchen. Daddy starts talking to Mummy.

'Yesterday afternoon in front of the TV went really well. I think Noah understands Watford's place in the world now – which means he's ready to go to his first match.'

When Noah hears this, he feels he's going to burst.

He doesn't want to give up his hiding place, though. So he shouts silently at his Lego footballer: 'Deeeneeyy!'

'But what if Watford win? Won't that scupper your plans for

your son's psychological health?'

Mummy says this to Daddy in the voice she uses when Daddy says she's being something called passive-aggressive.

'Watford won't win,' Daddy says. 'We've consistently lost to the big clubs: City, Arsenal, and now United. I'm going to take him to the Liverpool game.'

Liverpool! Noah is completely beside himself.

He scrambles out from under the table. He runs out through the open patio door.

He shouts 'Do not scratch your eyes!' and jumps into a flowerbed.

* * *

Noah is too excited to sleep. He lies in bed and thinks.

The Liverpool game is on Sunday, December 20. Daddy says Watford's next game after that is on Boxing Day. So if Santa is going to deliver in time for Christmas Day, Santa will have to make Watford win the Liverpool match.

Noah wriggles with excitement. Watford will beat a big club in the Premier League. And he'll be there to see it.

PART TWO

On the next three Saturdays, Daddy tells Noah that Watford have lost to Norwich, Aston Villa and Sunderland.

'The Liverpool game could make it four on the trot,' Daddy says.

There's something in Daddy's voice that doesn't sound entirely gloomy.

* * *

During the week, Daddy and Noah play football in the living room with a rolled-up sock. Daddy is in goal. Noah is trying to be Odion Ighalo, but he can't stop thinking about the Liverpool game on Sunday.

'Don't get your hopes up for a win, little guy,' Daddy says. 'Liverpool are a very big club. I'll be happy enough if we play well and lose.'

Noah boots the sock towards goal. Daddy lets it go through his legs. It looks a bit 'accidentally on purpose', but Noah doesn't mind. He sings the Ighalo song Daddy taught him.

Daddy says: 'And if we do beat Liverpool, Noah, it won't change anything. We'll still be the little guy. We always will be.'

Noah is puzzled. 'Little guy' is what Daddy calls Noah, and what Noah calls his Lego footballer. But Daddy is a big guy. So is Odion Ighalo. How can all of them be the little guy?

Noah stops puzzling and reminds himself he's Ighalo against Liverpool. He boots the sock past Daddy again.

He runs over to the lamp stand in the corner. He drops to his knees, looks up, and points both hands to the ceiling.

Of all the things Daddy has taught him about Watford, he likes this the best.

* * *

On Occupation Road, Noah holds Daddy's hand tight. He's never seen so many people in one place.

Daddy helps Noah through a turnstile. They go down some steps. It's quite dark. Noah sees bright light coming from a gap beside a snack bar. Daddy leads Noah into the gap.

Noah feels his eyes widening at the sight ahead of him. He sees a hilly white roof at the top. He sees a green rectangle at the bottom. He sees swirling yellow and black shapes in between. He can feel his heart beating very fast.

When they're through the gap, the noise hits them. Noah wants to cover his ears. But he doesn't dare let go of Daddy's hand.

Noah and Daddy sit down in their seats. The match kicks off. Daddy says into Noah's ear: 'Remember, little guy, we don't expect to win.'

Straightaway, Watford get a corner. Noah doesn't really see what happens. Suddenly Daddy jumps out of his seat. Noah puts his hands over his ears. Daddy picks Noah up, hugs him, and jumps up and down. Noah isn't sure why.

When it's quieter, Daddy explains to Noah what happened.

'Enjoy the feeling while it lasts,' Daddy says.

But soon after Daddy says this, Noah sees Odion Ighalo get the ball and smash it into Liverpool's net. Noah jumps out of his seat even faster than Daddy. Noah hugs Daddy's legs. Daddy and Noah jump up and down together.

When they sit back down again, Daddy has a tear running down his cheek.

'Always happens in the cold weather,' Daddy says.

Earlier in the afternoon, Daddy had told Noah it was very mild for the time of year. Noah doesn't think Daddy was lying. But he does start to think that perhaps Daddies don't always get things right.

* * *

At half-time, Noah listens in when Daddy is talking to the old man next to him.

'This is exactly what it was like when I was a kid,' Daddy says. 'We took on the big guys, dominated them, and beat them. Week after week. It was brilliant. Then, when I was twelve, it all stopped. Football taught me what our level really is.'

The old man next to Daddy says: 'Ah, but do we have a

real level? Deep down, I keep on thinking our level is lower division. But I'm in a minority now. Every generation sees it differently. It's all to do with where Watford are during your formative years.'

Noah looks at Daddy to see if Daddy is going to say something back. Daddy doesn't say anything. It looks like he's thinking.

The old man glances down at Noah. 'Who knows what level your little lad will grow up feeling we belong at? Today's level, maybe. You can't dictate it.'

Daddy turns and looks at Noah. Daddy still doesn't say anything.

The teams come out for the second half.

Everyone stands up and shouts.

* * *

On Occupation Road, Noah holds Daddy's hand tight again. This time, he's never seen so many people smiling. Watford have beaten Liverpool 3-0. Liverpool!

On the walk home, Noah asks Daddy: 'Are we still the little guy?'

Daddy looks at Noah for quite a long time before he answers.

'To be honest, I'm actually not sure we are.'

After that, Daddy stays very quiet. He seems to be thinking again.

* * *

It's past bedtime, but Noah is building an extra tier on his Lego stadium. He hears Daddy coming upstairs. He jumps into bed. Daddy sits on Noah's Watford duvet and looks down at Noah.

'I've got a confession to make, little guy. All season, up to today, I've been getting a lot of things wrong.'

Noah asks Daddy what things.

'It's hard to explain,' Daddy says. 'But one thing I've definitely been getting wrong is Watford's results.'

Daddy is holding the match programme he bought for Noah. He opens it on a page with lots of letters and numbers. Daddy says it shows Watford's results so far this season.

Daddy helps with some of the letters and explains how the numbers work. Together they go through all of Watford's results since the first match at Everton.

Noah is amazed. Watford didn't lose all their matches after all. They drew a few. Then they won a game. And another. And more still. With every victory, Noah shouts 'yes!' in a higher and louder voice. When Watford win at Stoke he hugs Daddy. When Watford win three games in a row against Aston Villa, Norwich and Sunderland, he starts bouncing on the bed.

Noah jumps into Daddy's arms and Daddy falls back onto the duvet. Noah lies on top of Daddy. Daddy shows Noah the league table in the programme. He explains where today's win over Liverpool has put Watford. It's near the top.

'I'm sorry,' Daddy says.

Noah doesn't understand why Daddy says he's sorry. Going through the results has been like opening Christmas presents. Five days early.

Good old Santa.

'I'm sorry I made you think we hadn't won,' Daddy says.

'That's okay,' Noah says. 'We did win.'

Daddy smiles.

'That's a relief,' he says. 'I thought you'd be cross with me, little guy.'

A frown wrinkles Noah's soft forehead. This is another thing Daddy has definitely got wrong. Today Noah has been to

Vicarage Road for the first time. He's seen Watford beat a very big club.

He corrects his father.

He says: 'None of us are little anymore, Daddy.'

16

Do you ever wonder what might have happened had the Pozzo family not purchased the club in summer 2012?

Channelling his inner pessimist, **Lionel Birnie** takes a trip to a parallel universe to find out...

SLIDING DOORS

BY LIONEL BIRNIE

That sound you heard as you walked down Occupation Road was the noise of coppers rattling and resentment.

Fans who dug deep to buy season tickets and replica shirts skimmed the change in their pockets and tossed it into the buckets as they headed towards the turnstiles.

'Fighting for our future,' shouted one of the bucket-shakers.

'Save our Hornets,' shouted another.

Watford were stuck in a loop. Exactly ten years after their last brush with armageddon, they were back here again, staring over the edge of the cliff at the jagged rocks below, hoping someone – anyone – would swoop in at the last moment to rescue them.

'What's Sir Elton doing these days?' said a fan as he threw a few quid into the bucket. 'Can't he do another concert?'

'He's bailed us out more than once before,' said his mate. 'Can't expect him to keep doing it.'

'I'd do it if I had his money.'

2012-13

At least there was a match on to take everyone's minds off the turmoil. Wycombe Wanderers, freshly relegated to the bottom division, were the visitors for a League Cup tie. The ground was almost empty – barely 4,000 souls clicked through the turnstiles that warm August afternoon.

The start of a new season offers the chance to dream, even when logic suggests that there's going to be little to celebrate, but this summer had been traumatic. Just about the only thing to put a smile on anyone's face was the cheerful logo of the club's new shirt sponsors, The Happy Egg Company.

And no one was smiling after 120 minutes of mostly tedious football either. Watford's best chance came in extra-time when a cross from the right fell to Chris Iwelumo, who made an unconventional connection with part of his shin that seemed destined to send the ball over the line, only for the Wanderers keeper to get a hand to it and push it over the bar. Watford lost the tie on penalties and the supporters trudged home afterwards thinking there could be a long, cold winter ahead. An ice age, perhaps.

For legal reasons the full story of the summer of 2012 still can't be told but here's what we do know. Laurence Bassini, the club's owner was locked in negotiations with the Russo brothers, Jimmy and Vince, over the ownership of the club. Lord Michael Ashcroft was still in the background too, determined not to lose out on his investment, but it was clear that Watford desperately needed new blood at the top to keep its heart beating. The running costs dwarfed the appetite or ability to keep pumping money in. The debt was rising like the totaliser on Comic Relief night, except no one was laughing.

There was an incident with the safe; long, fractious phone conversations; meetings scheduled and then cancelled at short notice; and a sense that not even the calming influence of Graham Taylor could sort this one out.

* * *

There had been one approach to buy the club, from the wealthy Pozzo family, owners of Udinese in Serie A, who had made a fortune selling their power tools company to Bosch and wanted to expand their football business empire to England.

Despite everything, the Pozzos were keen. They had a look round the stadium and, although unimpressed by the state of disrepair, could see potential. They looked at the books and saw past the obvious signs of a failing business and wondered what a quick injection of cash could do to reinvigorate the team. How much, Gino wondered, would it cost to get into the Premier League? Forty million? Fifty? Either way, it would be worth it.

Bassini promised to take Gino for a proper British pub lunch to discuss the deal further. He owned a pub, he said, opposite the ground, but they didn't do food at lunchtimes so he'd book somewhere else.

Gino Pozzo was unimpressed by the choice offered by the salad bar at the Harvester restaurant in Croxley Green. Bassini went back for seconds, covering everything in thick thousand island dressing.

'Great, isn't it,' he said, crunching on his bacon bits and iceberg lettuce.

'You can get here from the ground in ten minutes – even on matchday. And there's plenty of parking.'

Gino twirled the soggy, over-cooked spaghetti round the prongs of his bent fork, chewed the pap into a paste, dabbed at the corners of his mouth and excused himself from the table for a moment. He headed in the direction of the gents but swerved for the exit door at the last moment, dropping his shoulder like a footballer he owned called Forestieri. Gino climbed straight into his Maserati, set the sat-nav for Floyd Road, Charlton, south-east London, and drove away, taking his family's millions with him.

It was a good 20 minutes before Bassini realised Gino wasn't coming back.

* * *

On transfer deadline day, there were no positive updates from London Colney. All the business was being conducted elsewhere and the only news coming out of Watford was gloomy. The fans would come to think of it as Black Friday. Watford's chief assets had plunged in value because of the club's desperation to swap them for whatever money they could get. The final score when the markets closed? Troy Deeney to Derby County for £1.6million; Martin Taylor to Sheffield Wednesday for an undisclosed fee, Jonathan Hogg to Middlesbrough for next to nothing.

That left Sean Dyche with a skeleton squad of 15 professionals and a handful of kids.

But the killer blow came a couple of weeks after the transfer window had closed. The money raised was not enough and Watford were given a week to come up with £7million or face administration.

Administration, one of the dullest words in the English language, conjuring up images of filing paperwork and tax returns, is actually a terrifying one in football's lexicon. There's nothing tedious or perfunctory about it, it offers frightening uncertainty. Entering administration is not like stepping through the wardrobe into a magical land like Narnia, it's like being banished to Siberia. Often it's not extinction, but somehow it's even worse. It spells a points deduction, relegation, stagnation and oblivion.

When it came, the court's judgement was swift. A grey-faced man from a grey-faced firm of accountants with a grey logo was appointed to run the club. Decisions were made with barely a thought of how they might affect the football team because the team was so low on the list of priorities. All that mattered was clearing the club's debts, repaying the creditors as much as possible and saving enough of the business to make it a going concern, all while vetting potential suitors and weeding out the blood-thirsty opportunists.

The football authorities acted just as swiftly and before the news had even been digested by the supporters, the Championship league table was adjusted to take into account the ten-point deduction. A reasonable start for Dyche's boys had seen them scrape two draws, at Crystal Palace on the opening day and at home to Birmingham, from the first four games. That meant Watford were 24th, bottom of the table, on minus-eight points, already four wins from safety.

* * *

The news barely registered at the time but the Pozzo family got their English football club when they agreed to purchase Charlton Athletic. The resentment from football fans was immediate and Watford supporters joined in the heckling. Charlton were cheating, plain and simple. They'd sold their club's long history and famous heritage for a few grubby euros and surrendered their identity to Italian owners. They may as well have called themselves Udinese B. Then the loan players started arriving – a dozen or more foreign players, some for ridiculous fees Charlton could no way justify. Don't worry, the rest of football said, it'll blow up in their silly faces soon enough. Just imagine what a mess they'll be in when all the loan players have to go back!

* * *

It was a miserable season. Sean Dyche tried to be upbeat. 'It's going to be difficult, we know that,' he said with his gravelly voice after a 5-1 defeat at Derby, notable only for Lloyd Doyley's second career goal. 'There's no money and we're ten points behind where we should be. It's like going into the boxing ring with one hand tied behind your back. We know we're going to take a beating some days but we'll give it our best and we'll try to land a few blows. We won't give up, because you never know what can happen in football.'

Dyche almost worked miracles but the points deduction was simply too much to overcome. His team built from loyal servants such as Doyley and John Eustace, hard-working triers such as Carl Dickinson, Joe Garner and Mark Yeates, and youngsters thrown in too soon and relied on too much. The occasional loan signing helped prevent the campaign turning into a total disaster and meant hope flickered into the new year.

The ownership saga dragged on for months but, just after Christmas, Watford finally fell into new hands – a consortium of businessmen fronted by a man who claimed to be a fan took over. The supporters tried to be optimistic but when the press release contained the words, 'we will be careful custodians, who are determined to ensure the club lives within its means,' it felt as if any ambition left at Vicarage Road had been sucked out with a straw. The fans' doubts were confirmed when the new chairman slipped up in an interview with the *Watford Observer* by referring to Graham Taylor as Gordon Taylor.

And then it was back to fretting about the future, and whether it was worth worrying about the fact that six of the eight new board members were property developers...

Relegation was confirmed at Millwall on a Tuesday night in mid-April. Is there anything more depressing than that? Watford's fans packed the upper tier of the stand behind the goal and filled the charcoal south London sky with songs first of optimism, then fatalism, then defiance.

As Dyche and the players applauded the supporters, held open their hands in apologetic gestures and thumped their chests, just over the heart and the club badge, the fans chanted:

'We'll be back, we'll be back, we'll be back,' followed by 'Champions! Champions!'

There was the odd berk who'd spent all season yelling that Dyche and the players were a disgrace, simply not fit to wear the shirt. They were the ones who couldn't understand why Watford's ragtag collection of journeymen and green-round-the-chops kids could lose to Charlton, who'd signed 20 million quid's worth of talent for peanuts. The fans, well, most of them, recognised effort when they saw it. They tolerated the occasional hammering, they weathered the attritional goalless draws with good humour and they celebrated the unlikely wins when they came along. The crowds were thinning out but somehow that brought those who remained closer together. The football was boring most of the time, but it was character-building.

And when the final table was analysed, it turned out that, had they not been hit with the points deduction, the Hornets would have stayed up on goal difference. How very Watford.

2013-14

The crash woke the patients in Flaunden Ward at Watford General. It was just gone 4am and it sounded like the roof had caved in, which turned out to be the case, in a way. Fortunately, the hospital was still intact but the same could not be said about the main stand at Vicarage Road.

The old part, which was built in 1922, had been decrepit for almost a decade, derided as an eyesore and the standing embodiment of a football club in decline. Ambitious plans to redevelop the east side of the ground had been drawn up at intervals over the years and then shelved, despite the club twice submerging their faces in the Premier League's pot of honey.

Investigators came at first light to inspect the damage and quickly worked out that mice had chewed their way through one of the support beams, bringing the whole lot down.

The authorities issued the order to flatten the remains of the stand and over the summer the directors debated what to do with the space. Constructing a new grandstand in its place was clearly way beyond the club's means and so there were several entertaining suggestions. One was to put up 20-foot high advertising boards running the length of the pitch. 'It'll give the fans in the Rous Stand something to look at when the match is boring,' quipped one director.

'We could move the Hornets Shop hut up from the bottom car park,' suggested another. This idea was dismissed because the portacabin floor had a crack in it and they feared the thing might break in two if they tried to move it.

'How about a car park for VIPs?' The chief executive thumbed through his papers for a list of bookings for the coming season. 'Probably not necessary,' he said. 'Nobody important comes here anymore.'

'More flats?'

'Yes, terrific idea. More flats. Make sure there are patio doors for the ground floor flats that look out onto the pitch so the residents can watch the match. They've got something similar at Luton and it works a treat.'

And so construction work on a block of flats running the length of the touchline and backing onto Occupation Road began in June with residents promised they could move in by Christmas if they purchased a half-season ticket when they put down their deposit.

* * *

Back in what is now called League One for the first time since 1998, it didn't take long for a Lower Division pallor to settle over the club. Everything was just a bit more small-time and hand-to-mouth than it had been for a couple of generations.

The naming rights to Vicarage Road were flogged off to a local pawnbrokers for a cut-price rate and so Watford prepared to welcome their visitors to the Cash It In Stadium, which seemed somehow appropriate.

Few could blame Sean Dyche for not wanting to stick around. The job hed'd done had not gone unnoticed. Burnley had been after him for ages but he had refused to bail out on the Hornets until he'd exhausted his efforts to keep them up.

Watford's fans drew up a shortlist of wholly unrealistic targets to replace him. Gianfranco Zola (as if!), Neil Warnock (please no) and Alan Curbishley (naturally), but in the end the club went for Graham Westley of Stevenage, mainly because they wouldn't have to pay him relocation expenses.

Westley promised hard work, commitment and more hard work and a bit more commitment, and warned that anyone who didn't subscribe to his twin ideals of hard work and commitment would be joining the queue at the Job Centre.

When the fixtures came out, reality bit hard. Yes, there were a few lumbering giants in League One – Wolves, Sheffield United, Coventry City and perhaps half a dozen more that Watford had faced in slightly more glamorous circumstances. But it was the trips to Carlisle and Shrewsbury, Crawley Town and Stevenage that would chill the bones, especially as they were all scheduled for Tuesday nights in December and January.

There was also something called the Johnstone's Paint Trophy, which no big clubs were allowed to even enter.

Westley brought in a host of new players – committed, hard-working types who'd Done A Job For Him in the past. Every other match was a hard-fought draw and Watford settled into a mid-table groove that, try as they might, they couldn't claw their way out of.

At least the Thingy Paints Cup offered a bit of excitement –

and the prospect of a trip to Wembley. As Watford sailed through the early rounds (beating AFC Wimbledon and Dagenham & Redbridge) cup fever didn't so much take hold as leave everyone with a slightly irritating cough.

The cup run almost came to grief at Newport County. Persistent rain turned to a deluge midway through the second half. The ball stopped rolling and began skimming over the surface like a stone on the waves. The ref, who was from somewhere in the Midlands, had spent almost six hours on the M5 to get to the game and he didn't want to go through that again. Every time the ball splashed out of play, the ref batted away suggestions from the players that he abandon the game. He was committed to pressing on to 90 minutes, through extra time and penalties, even if he had to issue 22 sets of water wings to the players.

And then the floodlights went out, possibly because the torrential rain had got into the system and shorted the circuit, or more likely because Newport's kit man had flicked a switch on the instruction of the two managers.

The match was postponed twice more because of bad weather before Watford finally hammered a young, inexperienced Newport side 1-0 in extra-time.

The draw for the Southern Area Semi-Finals was conducted on Sky's Soccer AM programme one Saturday morning by presenter Helen Chamberlain and a bloke with a haircut from a band. The haircut supported Manchester United and made a funny face as he drew the balls from the barrel. What strange and exotic places these were – Swindon, Accrington, Chesterfield, Colchester. Then, a flicker of recognition as he drew Watford to face Portsmouth at the Cash It In stadium.

Pompey's chimes were silenced, then the Posh of Peterborough were brought down to earth over two legs and all of a sudden Watford were on their way to a first match under the giant arch at Wembley. A resounding 3-1 win over Chesterfield in front of almost 37,000 people gave Watford their first piece of silverware since the Second Division title was won on the banks of the Thames in May 1998. Several supporters were injured later that night jumping into The Pond because they hadn't realised it had been dredged dry as part of the council's elaborate gentrification programme.

A Wembley final and a tin pot for the sideboard took the sting out of a deeply underwhelming league campaign.

Watford finished 16th, having drawn a record 23 of their 46 games (11 of them 0-0). As foundations for a promotion push go, you can't get much more solid than that…

2014-15

Watford failed to win any of their first ten league games – equalling the worst start to a season in the club's history set in 2006-07. In fairness, Aidy Boothroyd's side had been in the Premier League, up against some of the best sides in the country (and Fulham). Graham Westley's side were beaten by Crewe, Fleetwood and Yeovil, among others, and at the end of September the manager did the decent thing and resigned, admitting he had taken the club as far as he could, which was technically true because the team were bottom of the table and could go no lower (at least until the end of the season).

There was shock when former favourites such as Andy Hessenthaler, Nigel Gibbs and Neal Ardley were overlooked for the job and, just as Hornets supporters thought it couldn't get any worse, Neil Warnock was unveiled as the new boss.

'Me missus was fed up with me moping round the house,' said Warnock, 'and I'm not much of a gardener, so I thought why not? Let's face it, I can't do any worse, can I?'

But Watford could do worse and Warnock's bullet-proof

self-confidence took a dent as Watford slipped to defeat after defeat. In November, the Hornets suffered their biggest cup humiliation since losing to Northwich Victoria in 1977 when they were bundled out of the cup by Hemel Hempstead Town at Vauxhall Road. 'We're the pride of Hertfordshire,' sang the Hemel fans as the Watford players trooped off the quagmire of a pitch.

The only bright spot in a miserable season came when Lloyd Doyley made his 504th first-team appearance, breaking Luther Blissett's record but, from the New Year onwards, Watford's hopes of avoiding relegation to the bottom division faded to nothing.

On April 29 – exactly 40 years to the day since Watford had last been relegated to the bottom division, then known as the Fourth Division – the Hornets' fate was sealed. In 1975 it was a defeat against Walsall that consigned Watford to relegation and a scarcely believable coincidence meant it was the Saddlers who did for them again. On a spring evening in the Midlands, an old friend was there to witness the demise. Troy Deeney, now worshipped by Derby supporters, was at Walsall's Bescot Stadium to see his two former clubs play. With a baseball cap pulled low over his eyes, he watched as the Hornets battled in vain to avoid the drop. After the game, as he walked against the flow of travelling supporters, he lost count of the number of people who wanted to shake his hand, slap him on the back and tell him, 'Come back and sort out this mess, Troy.'

2015-16

For an inanimate object, the fixture computer sure had a perverse sense of humour. The opening game of the League Two season, on Saturday, August 8, 2015 would be Luton Town versus Watford.

It would be the first meeting between the two clubs for ten seasons – the last being a 1-1 draw at Vicarage Road in the Championship on April 9, 2006.

To make matters worse (or better, depending on your point of view) the draw for the first round of the League Cup paired number 32, Luton Town, with number 48, Watford, to be played at Kenilworth Road on Tuesday, August 11, 2015. Two trips to the Kennel in four days. Someone was having a joke at the Hornets' expense.

In the days leading up to the first game, The Hornets Shop was doing a roaring trade in T-shirts. The most popular seller was a black number with the date 4.10.97 in yellow on the chest – although street traders in Vicarage Road were outselling them two-to-one with T-shirts bearing the sarcastic slogan 'We Love Colin' on the front.

The first game was an incendiary occasion, recalling memories, for those old enough, of the opening day of the 1993-94 season when Barry Ashby and Jason Drysdale were sent off during Glenn Roeder's first game in charge. That game had been open warfare on the pitch as two teams pumped up by the start of a new campaign, and a referee ill-equipped to cope with all the testosterone that entailed, lost control. This game was similar. There were crunching tackles and a 22-man brawl, as was traditional in the old days. The fans spat insults at each other and the small town rivalry of two clubs going nowhere at least took on some meaning. Watford thoroughly outplayed the Hatters and lost 2-1. For the contorted faces in the Oak Road end there was something perversely comforting about that.

A few days later, the atmosphere was just as fiery but the number of people who could be bothered with the cup was significantly fewer and so the anger on both sides seemed even more futile, like a queue of people waiting at a bus stop howling at the moon. Watford at least got the better of the enemy that night but there were to be no T-shirts celebrating the victory, even though it would turn out to be one of the more fondly remembered days in modern history.

Each year would feel like four seasons of winter from now on and the Hornets faithful wrapped up warm and hoped for a miracle to change their fortunes. It took a while but the crowds slowly slipped away and attendances were now down to four figures. A midweek game against Morecambe attracted the first sub-5,000 crowd for a league match since a 2-0 win over Oxford in November 1991.

Mothers and fathers who'd lived through the bad old days told their sons and daughters this was nothing new, that it was a supporter's duty to love the club unconditionally, through thick and wafer-thin. But the younger generation did not have the patience for a Sisyphean battle, and so they headed to Wetherspoon's to watch Chelsea on TV.

Summer 2016

It started as a rumour in the newspaper. The Pozzo family were thinking of selling Charlton Athletic and had their eyes on another club in the London area. It wasn't that things hadn't worked out at Charlton, it was more that the supporters were an ungrateful bunch. They couldn't get used to the high turnover of players and the annual change of head coach. They craved stability, like in the old days.

Gino Pozzo thought back to his trip to Hertfordshire. He'd had a good feeling about Watford the first time he'd visited.

The deal was done quickly and, having sold Charlton to the Chinese, there was plenty of money to drag Watford out of League Two and up through the divisions. The first signing was a midfielder – a Swiss international with a great touch and an eye for goal.

OTHER BOOKS IN THE SERIES

TALES FROM THE
VICARAGE

VOLUME 1
VOLUME 2
VOLUME 3: THE INTERVIEWS
VOLUME 4

Brilliant original stories about Watford FC
by journalists, fans and former players.

All books in the series are available now from
talesfrom.com

Also available from the Hornets Shop at Vicarage Road,
Amazon and other major retailers.